COURAGE
IN
CRISES

BEYOND ABUSE,
ANGER AND ADDICTION

James Brown

Foreword by
Les Brown

LT
Life Tree Publishing
ATLANTA, GEORGIA

This book chronicles the life and times of the author. While the people, places and incidents are real, based on the author's recollection of facts, some names and places have been changed to protect identities.

ISBN 978-0-9777278-2-7

Library of Congress Control Number: 2007932236

Edited by Annette R. Johnson, editor@e-allwrite.com

DEDICATION

I would like to dedicate this book in memory of *M.C. "Pop" Bailey*, my uncle and best friend. He was the umbilical cord to my destiny. I would also like to dedicate this book to *Mrs. Hooper*, my 1st grade teacher, for believing in me; *Tommy Brown*, my father, for teaching me that no one is ever going to give you anything in life. "If you want it," he said, "you have to go out and get it"; *Les Brown* for saying, "You don't have to be great to get started, but you have to get started to be great!" He made this cripple boy jump out of his hospital bed and begin fulfilling his destiny; and *Lakisha Tanksley*, a young lady who Les Brown introduced me to and who died suddenly of breast cancer before we were to start writing this book, for reminding me to do things in the spirit of excellence. Now, partial proceeds from this book will go to find a cure for breast cancer and spinal cord injuries. Finally, I would like to thank *Candice Ellis* for helping me to compose my thoughts.

FOREWORD

James Brown does more confined to a wheelchair to make a difference in this world than most people will do in a lifetime standing up and moving around. Brutally raped at a tender age, taunted, teased and humiliated by his peers, paralyzed by age 21, and exploited by many – even in the church – yet none of these things were tragic enough to rob James of his passion as he sets out on a mission to change the lives of our youth.

Coming from such a tragic past, one would agree that James has every right to be angry, bitter and hopeless, but that is not the case. His life is a testament to Robert Schuller's quote that says, "If life gives you lemons, make lemonade."

Confined to a wheelchair but not confined in his thinking, James believes we can and ought to be a driving force in the lives of our youth. At a time when so many people are writing off many of our youth who are suffering from HIV (hood infected virus), addiction to death, and incarceration syndromes, James is a voice in the urban wilderness crying, "There is hope!"

At one of my speaker training seminars, we marveled at him in his rotating wheelchair being among the first in the room and the last to leave. He is always on a quest to improve his communication skills so that he can make a greater impact on his young audiences. In fact, when James speaks, the passion in his voice permeates the whole room. He ignites the power in you that compels you to positive action.

James' book, *Courage in the Midst of Crises*, is ultimately a handbook of how to live a life of freedom from your past and greater promise for your future. It's a book about courage, forgiveness and grace. Motivational speaker Dennis Gardner says, "It does not matter what happens to you in life; it is what you do about it." Life moves on all of us. James walks us through the process of how you and I, in using his example, can strengthen our minds and spirits to overcome the storms of life, which are inevitable.

Our children are the future leaders of this world, and James' book emphatically demonstrates that it is incumbent on all of us to do our part to create a brighter tomorrow. Even without the use of his feet, he has taken the first step, and now James is inspiring us to step out, step up and do our part!

Les Brown

TABLE OF CONTENTS

PROLOGUE

I'm far from the boy I once was, but not yet the man I strive to be. Every day I move further away from my past, learning how to keep only what I need to move forward. My life has been a series of unusual and unimaginable episodes. Still, I remain motivated to stay on a path of improvement and to make each phase of my life better than the one before. By reliving my life within these pages, I hope to share the lessons I've learned. I'll start my story where most begin: childhood.

CHAPTER ONE

UNSPOKEN WORDS

I'll always remember my mother's warning about being too open about our household. True, at times I was a talkative child, but my chattiness came more from a desire to be noticed than a desire to spread family business. My elementary school teachers routinely commented that I was a good student but talked a little too much. Unlike adults who have learned to doctor the truth, most young children tell the unadulterated truth. At 6, I was no different. Ms. Hooper, my first-grade teacher, had sent a note home. I don't know what she wrote, but I'll never forget my mother's words. "Stop telling our business," she would say. "Don't you know what goes on in your house stays in your house?"

Little did my mother know that those words would characterize my existence. As she instructed, I stopped talking – until now.

I attended J.H. House Elementary School in Conyers, Georgia, where I live to this day. School was my escape, the place where I would pretend that nothing was wrong. Ms. Hooper was my favorite teacher. Secretly, I hoped I was her favorite student too. I loved Ms. Hooper because she made me feel special, as if what I had to say was important. I believe she knew there was something wrong, though I cannot be certain. I told her that my mother didn't work and that she would sit at home and watch soap operas. Somehow, my mother viewed discussions of our home life as an invasion of privacy, a concept I had not yet grasped.

I was born February 23, 1971, the youngest of three children. My brother, Thomas, was the oldest, and my sister, Carla, was the middle child. I was named after my father's cousin, who was a construction worker.

One day, while working in a trench where he was laying sewage pipes, the dirt collapsed on him, and he was buried alive. Like my namesake, ironically, I too felt buried alive. My home was not inviting, at least in my eyes. Year after year, it seemed the weight of my existence grew heavier.

Often, instead of feeling loved or wanted, I felt like an uninvited guest and would retreat to my room or some other quiet corner. I grew up in a three-bedroom house with my parents, Shirley and George Brown, and my siblings. I shared a room with my brother, but not much more. We did, however, both fear the dark but for different reasons. While he feared the dark itself, I froze whenever I saw the étagère or, according to my mother, the "whatnot." I could handle its commanding presence in the daytime, but at night, it became a "monster."

My brother was one year older than my sister and five years older than I. My brother and sister shared a bond, probably because of their close age; they were partners. I, however, was the odd man out. Uncle A.W., my mother's brother, rented the garage. He mingled with us occasionally, but he basically lived his own life. I don't think anyone realized the role he actually played, at least not until he left.

An equal opportunity abuser, my father showed no discrimination in dispensing his merciless brand of corporal punishment. "One Time," that's what I called him, though I dared not use the name in his presence. You had one time to mess up; then he would literally beat you down. There was no excuse for his actions, but I'm sure that the way he grew up affected him. My father had no idea who his father was. He grew up with a stepfather, who showed no mercy in discipline. He even shot his own brother for coming onto his property. Luckily, his brother survived, but he was sent to prison. Before his sentence ended, he was eligible for parole. However, my grandfather told the parole board he would shoot his brother again, so he was never released and died in prison.

My paternal grandmother did little to stop the pattern my father would repeat. My father's stepfather cursed at him all the time and rarely gave him anything. He had to pick cotton just to get a pair of pants for school. Even though my paternal grandparents lived less than a mile away from us, they seldom visited. On Christmas, my grandmother would drop off presents, but no hugs and kisses.

Even with his rough edges, my father always provided his family with the necessities. He was good with his hands and worked at Wilson Art until he got a job at General Motors, where he worked on an assembly line. He rarely splurged on himself, though he had a motorcycle. Despite this adornment, he was far from fashionable. Blue jeans and t-shirts were his standard attire. His biker friends called him "Georgia Trader." Buying, repairing, and selling junk cars were his hobbies and ways to make extra money.

Since my father worked 16-hour days, my mother was the main caregiver. While my brother and sister were at school, I would sit on the edge of her bed playing for hours it seemed. Toys were scarce, so I made my own. With a box of Crayola crayons, I created an imaginary world. Each color was a different personality. The black crayon was the man, a basketball superstar whom I wanted to be like. I would use a deodorant spray can nozzle as the ball and an old mayonnaise jar, which we drank from, as the goal. Other kids had plastic soldiers; I had crayons, toiletries and food packaging.

Colors and numbers fascinated me, and I enjoyed learning. My mother says when my brother and sister would come home from school, they would read to me, as well as teach me my alphabets, numbers, and writing. The childhood memories that linger most are of my mother reading to me, telling stories of far away lands that were nothing like the world where I lived.

Because my mother couldn't drive, we rarely ventured outside of the house or yard. She was and still is a simple, yet intelligent woman, meeker than her husband. Maybe he looked for these qualities. Her mother died when she was 7. My mother said that my grandmother, a maid, went to work one day and never came home. She apparently had an aneurysm in her brain. It wasn't easy for her father and three brothers to teach a girl how to be a woman. Thus, they sought the help of her grandmother and did the best they could. By the time she was 19, my grandfather had died too.

Handling the bills was my mother's responsibility, so my father gave her his paycheck. She could make a dollar stretch until it screamed for mercy. To save money, she always pressed her own hair. My mother re-used everything that she could, even her clothes. I'll never forget her floral printed dress. The flowers had long lost their bloom, but she wore it like a uniform.

We ate black-eyed peas, butter beans, okra, Vienna sausages, and potted meat galore. Kool-Aid, Chek soda, and Frosted Flakes were con-sidered treats. She wasn't the best cook, but we never went hungry. "One Time" forbade us from leaving food on our plates. I often tempted fate and mashed my food under the table. Leftovers, aside from what we saved for my dog, Lucky, were rare. Even Lucky was a bargain. He was a plain yard dog, no special breed, but special to me.

Our house was in a wooded area. Most would call it country. In fact, it wasn't uncommon to see cows nearby. Our back yard was filled with plum trees. More than the sweet taste of those plums, though, I most re-member the sting of the tree branches hitting against my skin whenever my parents disciplined me. Our parents only allowed us to play on our own property, so we didn't get to regularly interact with other children unless we were at school. Ignoring the consequences, I would sometimes boldly go to my next-door neighbor's house. We'd ride our bikes in a circle or play catch football. When my mother would look outside and see me, she would make me pick a sufficient-sized switch from a tree so she could spank me. Even my brother and sister longed to cross the grass boundaries that separated our yard from the others, step onto the concrete driveway, go into the street, or simply play with the neighborhood chil-dren. That's why we enjoyed our visits to Aunt Janice's.

Aunt Janice, my father's aunt, lived a few streets away. Visiting her house was a treat for our mom and us. "Goin' up to Rena Court. We're goin' up the street," we'd chant when my mother told us it was time to leave. We relished those weekends because Janice had four adopted kids, and the children's friends always came to her home to play. Playing "Hide and Go Seek," "1-2-3 Red Light," and "Mother, May I" took on new life at Janice's. While she sat in the house or on the porch with my mother, we felt free.

One day my aunt told my male cousin to go out to the tool shed in the back yard. He was 16, and I felt privileged when he asked me to accompany him. My brother and sister, I sensed, did not want to be bothered with a baby, particularly when they had their pick of other kids to play with. Eagerly, I walked with him to the shed. As soon as we entered, he locked the door and told me to go over to a corner to get a hammer. "I don't see no hammer," I said, afraid that I wasn't helping him at all. Then, from the corner of my eye, I saw him go over to a dresser and reach for some Vaseline.

Instinctively, I knew something was not right. "I don't see no hammer! I don't see no hammer!" I said, frantically looking around. That's when he grabbed me, pulled my pants down and started rubbing Vaseline on me. I screamed, and he told me to shut up as he covered my mouth. Then I felt his penis inside my rectum. I tried to pull away, but his grasp was too strong. He continued to cover my mouth with one hand while pressing me against him with the other. Finally, he released me. Tears rolled down my face as I tried to comprehend what had just happened. "Shut up," he said. "Don't tell nobody. If you do, you'll get in trouble. Stop. Stop. Stop all that crying. You better not tell anybody."

He unlocked the door and told me to leave the shed. Then, he went on his way. I sat on the ground near the shed, not moving or saying a word. It seemed like an hour had passed. It was about 6 p.m. when my brother came looking for me. It was time to go. Pain replaced the feelings of exuberance I usually experienced during the walk home from Aunt Janice's. I looked at my brother, my mother, and my sister as they walked in front of me, but I remained silent. I went home and mechanically went through the motions of my nightly routine. I sat in my room, crying on the inside and thinking about what my cousin had done to me. I couldn't go to my mother. She had already told me that I talked too much. I couldn't go to my father because he might have beaten me. That night and for years to come, I kept my thoughts to myself. At 6, I had begun to learn the power of words, especially those unspoken.

COURAGE IN CRISES

CHAPTER TWO

LIVING IN TIME OUT

Before that Saturday, my biggest fear was the étagère in our living room. To me, it was big, tall, and monstrous. Now, however, I knew real-life monsters existed.

The next morning, I went to Sunday school and church. Getting the kids ready on Sundays was my father's job. "You better get your ass up out that bed and get ready for church," he'd say. Even though he didn't work on Sundays, he wouldn't come with us. We never understood why, and we never asked. Only my father's own funeral could get him into church, and one day it did.

Because my mother couldn't drive, my grandmother's brother Alphonso, or A.W., always drove us to church. He would give us a dollar for the offering and a dollar to keep. I looked forward to my dollars, particularly the one I kept. Some Sundays, my father dropped us off at the Laundromat. My mom washed the entire household's clothes, including A.W.'s. While she waited for the clothes to dry, we walked to the corner store. There we spent Uncle Alphonso's money on sugary treats: cinnamon buns, Dr. Pepper, and Tootsie Rolls. A dollar went a long way in those days.

My grandfather built the church we attended, New Hope Baptist Church, shortly after he joined the congregation in 1955. He had only a third grade education, but people say that when he spoke, he sounded like he had a college education. In fact, I've never heard anyone say anything bad about him, and my family has always been notorious for ridiculing people. He had a stellar reputation and a big heart, which was evidenced in the fact that he built the new building for free because the old church was dilapidated.

Many members of my extended family attended and participated in the church services. My Aunt Rhett sat in the back along with the other ushers who always had switches ready to discipline children who misbehaved. We had two preachers. One stuttered, and the other was long-winded. Church lasted three to four hours. Boring and long, that was my perception of the services. Despite the hooping and hollering of the Spirit-filled, I typically slept in church. Needless to say, biblical concepts escaped me. This Sunday, though, I needed to talk to God. In fact, he was the only one I talked to. "Why did my cousin have to do that to me?" I asked. The question remained unanswered.

My body ached, but no one knew. Four people lived with me, but still I was alone. For most of my childhood, loneliness was a constant companion. Displays of affection were infrequent. One Time raised us to be tough, so my brother, sister, and I didn't hug each other. I'm sure they must have, but I never saw my parents hug, kiss, or dance, for that matter. At dinner time, they took their plates to their bedroom while we remained at the table. They argued often, and I suppose that was their way of communicating. For most of my young life, my family avoided talking about important issues. We somehow coexisted without delving into each other's lives.

Our inability to talk and to truly communicate hurt me deeply. In particular, I wanted to spend quality time with my father. I wanted him to give me the same attention he gave his cars. On weekends, I gazed out the window towards the driveway and saw him repairing the cars. As I watched, I fantasized that we were playing ball or going places together. I knew my father was capable of showing love and interest. Otherwise, how could he have won my mother's heart?

My parents met in middle school and became high school sweethearts. My mother was an eighth-grader and a year older than my dad. She said her attraction to him wasn't immediate. The more my father tried to woo her, the more she regarded him as a pest. Eventually, my father's efforts succeeded. They dated and had my siblings. On July 1, 1967, less than a month after my sister's birth, my parents married. Their union was mainly based on necessity as well as love. Fresh from Air Force basic training, my father thought he might die in Vietnam, so he wanted to ensure that he provided for his family.

It saddens me that I only knew the postwar version of my father, an incessantly angry man. According to my mother, Vietnam changed him mentally and physically. Perhaps these changes allowed her to excuse his behavior. The trauma of seeing so many people die, friends and enemies, hardened my father even more. In addition to the trials of his childhood, the horrors of war further darkened my father's thoughts. When his four-year enlistment ended, he returned to civilian life. My father brought home two unwanted souvenirs: post-traumatic stress disorder and the side effects of Agent Orange.

I longed for my father to hug me or to tell me he loved me. I loved him, but I disliked his ways at the same time. I knew my mom liked me, but due to my parents' distant behavior, I wondered if they loved me. By going to work and providing a home, food, and clothing for their children, my parents thought they had fulfilled their parental duties. For me, words of encouragement meant as much as all those things. As a family, we were disconnected, and that would become more evident in time.

Initially, I had no apparent physical signs of molestation. However, the first time I had a bowel movement after the incident, I couldn't control it. Being a bed-wetter, my insecurities grew. While I tried not to, I became overly sensitive, crying constantly. A stern glance from my father was enough to trigger tears. My brother and sister already teased me the way siblings do. Though they weren't cruel, I became more of a loner, afraid of the teasing that soiling my pants might bring. My problem followed me to school. Despite the definite possibility that my classmates might make fun of me, I never missed a day.

Before I started using the bathroom in my pants, I faced Sammy White. Each morning, my mother stood at the front door, watching me board the bus. Sammy greeted me almost every day. He looked like a wolf and acted like one too. Sammy wore his long black hair slicked back and quickly charged at anyone who dared sit in one of "his" back seats. Fighting thrilled him. Still, I viewed Sammy as a nuisance rather than a threat. Oddly enough, he rarely spoke at school, and we attended the same church. When Sammy hit, I hit back. When he pushed, I pushed back with more force. Big for my age, strangers frequently mistook me for an older child. Size proved to be an advantage when I dealt with Sammy. Later, it would protect me from my schoolmates' taunts.

I tried to make it to the restroom, but rarely did. Accidents ruined my entire day. I sat in my wet, soiled clothes until I got home. My schoolmates called me "doo-doo man," "stinky booty baby," and every possible humiliating combination they could conceive. I was already self-conscious due to my size and limited wardrobe. I was a fat boy, the biggest kid in the class.

During my first-grade year, my mom started working in the accounting department at Sears. Since the store offered an employee discount, she bought our school clothes there. I rotated between a few pairs of husky-sized Toughskins, a couple of knockoff Izod shirts, and one pair of Zips sneakers. My mother walked two miles to and from her job, so leaving to pick me up was not an option. Zero possibility existed that my dad would leave his job early. Being the center of attention in class was a burden I had no choice but to bear. A latchkey kid, I sat at home by myself after school, waiting for my brother and sister. Normally, I hated being alone, but when I had a mishap, I welcomed the privacy. I felt like an outsider at school and at home.

Although my kindergarten teacher, Ms. Hooper, ignored my accidents, she sensed something was wrong. On good days, I relished participating in her class. She helped me realize my potential by nominating me to voice a character on "Wee Pals," a local cartoon. My family could care less that my voice was coming from the television on Saturday mornings. Alone I sat, week after week, watching the show. Ms. Hooper, on the other hand, acknowledged my accomplishment. Under her guidance, I flourished. She treated me with respect although I blurted out answers. I made good grades in part because I liked to learn and in part because I wanted to impress Ms. Hooper. "James, go to the chalkboard. Write it down," she often told me. Eagerly, I complied. On bad days, I wanted to be invisible. I slouched in my seat, hoping no one detected the smell coming from my pants. Nevertheless, others did notice, so Ms. Hooper sent a note home.

Ms. Hooper talked to me in the hallway that day. She tried to assess my situation. I think she wanted my parents to be aware of how my condition affected the class and me. Certainly, she recognized the abnormality of the circumstances. At home, my parents treated my problem as a lack of self-control. I wonder if a visit to the doctor would have exposed my secret. I'll never know because I never went. My parents reserved doctor visits for emergencies, like when I broke my collarbone after falling off the back of my brother's bike as we rode up the street. This happened before I was raped. Pooping in my pants didn't qualify as worthy of a doctor. "Wash out your drawers," my parents would say. Accusing me of being "lazy" offered a simple solution for why I pooped in my pants, so my parents felt justified when they beat me for it.

I knew misbehavior had its consequences. I learned this from going outside or leaving the yard without permission. Usually, my parents beat all of their children when one child got in trouble, regardless of the culprit. Sometimes, if we did something wrong in the daytime, my mother let us think we had gotten away with it. However, all was not forgotten. When One Time came home from work, he'd beat my brother, sister and me awake. Then, the three of us had to bend over the bed for more. He lit our butt up plenty of nights. My father's beatings caused more terror than my mom's. He used a leather belt but later upgraded to a one-inch strap that he thought would do a better job. I believe that strap could bring tears to a grown man's eyes. I accepted my punishment bravely even though I knew that my so-called laziness had nothing to do with my lack of desire. Instead, I had a genuine lack of ability.

As much as my father's strap hurt, he had a more powerful way of beating me down. Enduring my classmate's ridicule was difficult, but my father's words hurt the most. He interchangeably used "shit ass" and "knucklehead" in place of my name.

The sting of his words slowly diminished and hearing them became almost normal, but in my soul, I felt pain.

I begged to stay at home when my mother went to Aunt Janice's. Still, she made me go, but I kept close to my brother, sister or my mother. If I saw my cousin, I immediately became tense and went the other way. In fact, playing in solitude became more desirable for me. Riding my bike in circles in the yard or sitting on our porch playing "that's my car" wasn't so awful anymore. A little later, my cousin joined the military. Knowing he was miles away offered some relief. Gradually, I blocked out the rape. Even my accidents didn't remind me. Days faded into months, months faded into years.

As time passed, so did the distance between me and my siblings. Following in their footsteps was difficult, especially after I had been un-officially branded as the least likely to succeed. Carla, the angel, rarely did wrong. While in high school, she worked and spent time at her boyfriend's house. My father cosigned Carla's car loan, something he wouldn't consider doing for my brother or me. Carla's car provided her with a sense of freedom, and I envied her. When we were younger, Thomas instigated most of the mischief. Once, he boldly stole $100 from my father. "If ya'll don't find my $100, I'm gonna beat ya'll butt," yelled my father. Innocently, my brother searched along with me and my sister.

We thought we had searched everywhere, but then Thomas whispered to my sister, "Look under the rug." Of course, there lay the money. Our father beat us anyway. Despite his sticky fingers and mischievousness, Thomas' undeniable intellect intimidated me. He despised studying and bringing textbooks home but still did well enough to attend West Point. The opposite of me, Thomas was tall, slim, bow-legged, and had all the girls. His dimples and his smile hooked them. Moreover, being a star athlete in both football and track added to his popularity. As I got older, I wanted to be like him.

The teasing at school and the verbal abuse at home continued. Through it all, I remained focused on my studies. Besides learning in the class-room, I also enjoyed physical education. I anxiously awaited field day and prayed I didn't have an accident before or during an event. It was my opportunity to shine. Although I excelled in many events, especially the meter dashes, the softball throw proved to be my specialty. When the starting whistle blew, I ran as fast and as far as my Zips would take me. I won numerous ribbons for my athletic ability. I was a good athlete but not as good as Burt Harmon, who lived three houses down the street from me. Burt had natural talent; his movements appeared effortless. We met when I was six, and he became one of my closest friends. I wanted to be as fast as he, and his athleticism pushed me to be better.

Year after year, my interest in sports increased along with my size. Trying out for the football team was my goal. On Sunday afternoons, I watched NFL football and studied the plays. Conyers Middle School only allowed seventh and eighth graders to tryout, so I started preparing for my chance while in sixth grade. I gained more weight and, in the process, developed an aggressive attitude. Fighting my schoolmates protected me from the teasing. Word spread that when it came to "throwing blows," I showed no hesitation. Anything I perceived as a violation, even stepping on my shoes, set me off. Circumstances made me a bully of sorts, and I used physical force to protect myself emotionally.

I fought many times, but none were memorable except for my encounter with Ted Christian. He stepped on my first brand-name tennis shoes, a pair of Nikes that M.C. had given me the money to purchase. I pushed him, and he immediately pushed me back. The onlookers grabbed us, trying to prevent the inevitable. "Meet me in the bathroom after school," said Ted, suggesting that we fight there instead. He was bigger than I, but I met him in the bathroom without hesitation after sixth period. I don't know what came over me, but I football tackled him like a lion seeking his prey. I literally beat him down, and people had to pull me off him. After this, students started warning, "Don't mess with him. He's crazy." I wasn't crazy, though, just experienced. I had been fighting with my brother and against my daddy, so taking on a bigger opponent like Ted was nothing to me. I had gained lots of admirers at this point, but I wanted real friends – at least one.

While I was playing basketball in the gym my sixth grade year, I met Renaldo "Nard" Franklin. Nard told me he liked my style, and I liked his too. Besides, he could out talk me. Finding someone who could do that was rare. Always a jokester, Nard lifted my spirits. Every so often, he took his quips to another level, almost making me want to fight him. I considered Nard and Burt my best friends. Graciously, they overlooked my accidents. Nard and Burt frequently witnessed my temper flare-ups without experiencing them firsthand. They offered me their unconditional friendship and devotion.

Burt and I decided to tryout for the team together. Eventually, I persuaded Nard to do the same. He lived in the projects and saw football as a way out. I think we all dreamed of being professional athletes and escaping our mundane, small-town lives. More than anyone, even Nard, I felt I needed this opportunity. Through football, I'd gain acceptance and popularity. Instead of being a joke, I'd be a hero like Walter Peyton. I envied the way he ran the ball, his footwork, and his grace. Peyton danced on the field. Fans idolized his tenacity. I wanted what Peyton had, and I almost got it.

CHAPTER THREE

LEAVING TIME OUT

Scared, excited, confident, determined, many emotions coursed through my mind during football tryouts. Neither the scorching Georgia sun nor the sweat stinging my eyes could deter me, though. I fed on the adrenaline rush and proved to Coach Sellers that the team needed me as the nose guard. The position suited me, and I proudly wore number 62. But making the cut proved to be only the beginning. I had to show I was worthy of starting. Pecking order dictated that experienced players received more game time. In my mind, I was a star, but in actuality, I was a rookie. The first game humbled me because Coach Sellers allowed me on the field for only one short play. I had to reevaluate my status after warming the bench as other players battled on the field.

With strengthened determination, I sought to improve my performance. Thus, I continued taking my brother's protein mix. I'm sure he must have noticed his dwindling supply. Thoughts of the sport lulled me to sleep at night and consumed my waking hours. I also added viewing Monday Night Football to my regime. Huddled in front of my small black-and-white television set, I memorized moves. At practice, I defended the ball as if I were facing an actual opponent. From the sidelines I heard, "Go, J.B. Go. Hunker down, J.B." These words came from my teammates' fathers. They told me I was great at defending the ball, but I wanted to hear my dad's voice cheering me on. My mom came to the games, and when I saw her in the stands, part of me hoped my dad would be next to her.

Football became my therapy, a way to release the frustration I felt. A sanctioned form of fighting, football allowed me to raise hell. Finally, I had a chance to hit people and to receive praise instead of punishment. Tackling the quarterback or whoever had the ball was my purpose. Not only did I often keep the opponent from advancing, I also ensured that the opponent fell down hard. My game improved steadily in football, but my mother was the only person in my family who knew that.

More than my father's indifference towards me, his treatment of my mother disturbed me. Our home had become more volatile since the previous year. A.W. married his girlfriend, Lillian, and moved out. She was smart, caring, and the type of woman I dreamed of marrying. I missed A.W.'s presence. He taught me how to cut the grass, a chore my father fixated upon. He also taught me basic construction methods while building a new kitchen for the church. Without A.W.'s rent payment, our family's financial strain increased. My father seemed to become bolder and louder as a result. He cursed at my mother, and she cursed him back. Closed doors prevented me from seeing the abuse, but I heard the fights through the thin walls. At times, I crouched at my parents' bedroom door, fearing the worst. Hearing my father's fist pound against my mother's skin as she begged him to stop left me feeling powerless. I sat at the door with a butcher knife, prepared to help my mother if she needed me. I summoned the courage to knock on the door but never the courage to open it. I usually just went across the hall to my room, placed a pillow over my head, and waited for the noises to subside. One of my parents would come to my door and look around. Sometimes, they would stop fighting once they saw me. My siblings ignored the fights and me, but I had to take some type of action, however small.

Once, my mother emerged from her room with a black eye. Her attempts to mask the bruising with makeup failed. Still, we overlooked her condition. Reality paused in our home. We were actors, each aware of the evolving scene but focused solely on our own roles, careful not to overstep our bounds.

When I wanted to experience my ideal of family life, I walked to my uncle M.C.'s house. My mother's brother had a chuckle that started deep within his big belly, like Santa Claus. We talked, and most importantly, my uncle listened without dismissing my ideas. M.C. constantly gave me advice. We discussed sports and life in general. I never asked him to come to a game because of his hectic schedule, for he towed cars for a dealership and worked long hours. His wife, Alice, also worked. Nonetheless, they managed to make time for each of their seven children. I became their unofficial eighth child. Some paydays, my uncle gave his kids $20, and eagerly, I stood in line to receive my share. Without hesitation, M.C. would hand me a crisp bill.

On a weekly basis, I spent at least two days at his home. I savored Alice's cooking and often stayed for dinner. She made the best dressing. Not a Thanksgiving passed without me at her table. Spending the holiday at M.C.'s seemed right. I was thankful for my surrogate family.

In M.C.'s home, I found solace. In football, I found power. My intense concentration on the game paid off. Soon, Coach Sellers viewed me as an integral element of the Bulldog's success. No longer did I sit on the sidelines. Anxiously, I anticipated the annual football awards banquet.

At last, the evening came. I watched fellow teammates and their families filter into the room. None of my relatives came to support me, though. Even so, nothing could ruin this night. Surely, I'd be the most valuable seventh-grade player. I inched to the edge of my seat as the speaker announced the winner. It wasn't me. David Clay, a running back who didn't play as much as I did, stole my glory. Defeated and disheartened, I wondered why. I clapped when Dave received the most valuable seventh grade football player award, yet envious thoughts crept through my mind.

That evening, I replayed the past season in my mind. Dave must have won because of variables beyond my control. Could it be race? African-Americans comprised the minority in Rockdale County. Could it be economics? His parents donated to and participated in the booster club. After pondering numerous scenarios, I decided to ask Coach Sellers. His response surprised me. "You missed practice and needed to try harder," he said. Sellers' answer stung partly because it rang of truth. Sometimes I had difficulty finding a ride to practice. Other times, my father wouldn't let me go or made me leave early. "Get your ass home and cut that grass or you ain't gonna play football," he'd say. Every other day it seemed, my father insisted that my brother or I cut the grass. He called us "sorry" if we didn't cut it quickly enough or to his specifications. With my brother preparing to graduate and leave for the Army, grass cutting became my main chore. In hindsight, I should have appeased my dad and done everything possible to make it to practice. Although my passion for the sport showed on game nights, being absent from practice caused the coach to question my commitment.

Proving the coach wrong and becoming the school's biggest football star became my goal. My training schedule intensified. After practice, I ran up and down hills, and did extra pushups and sit-ups. In pre-game huddles, I fired up the team. On and off the field, I became more daring. Head-butting opponents and grabbing female schoolmates' behinds were frequent activities. Part bully, part football star, I looked for shortcuts to academic success. I coerced fellow students into doing my schoolwork while others volunteered. I looked forward to attending Jackson State University, Walter Peyton's alma mater. Somehow, I thought, I'd realize this goal, even as I relied on others to sustain my grades.

The boy who once rushed to the chalkboard found himself obsessed with two things: football and Erin Johnson. The moment I saw Erin, I set out to make her mine. Many of the teenage boys at my school lusted after Erin. Her petite frame, bowlegs, and sparkling white teeth attracted us. As she characteristically walked by on her toes, my eyes followed her every movement. At this point in my life, I knew little about the opposite sex. I especially didn't know how to treat a young lady, so I followed my father's lead. I took advantage of any and every opportunity to intimidate Erin. I followed her in the halls and lurked outside of her classes. "Oh, there goes James Brown's girl," students sarcastically remarked as I waited for Erin to emerge from class. I often hit Erin, grabbed her, and told her what she was going to do. An alpha male, I forcefully pressed my lips against hers, trying to imitate how I thought a kiss should feel. Each time I held her slender frame against mine, instead of feeling warmth, I felt the coldness of fear.

Erin didn't want to be my girl, but at least I had football. My proudest moment occurred in the second game of the season against Sharpe Middle School, our rivals who lived in Newton County, 20 minutes away. We played on their turf. With a score of 6-0, our eminent defeat loomed. The 4th quarter had 2 minutes left when they decided to punt. Defensive tackle Keith Beacon rushed in and blocked the punt, and I picked up the ball and ran 40 yards for the touchdown. The crowd roared, "J.B., J.B., J.B.!" We kicked the extra point, gaining a 7-6 lead. Then, we scored another touchdown after Matt Miner intercepted a pass, and I smashed one of Sharpe's players, allowing Miner to score. The crowd continued shouting my name. After kicking the extra point, we won 14-6. My teammates' parents bounded from the stands, commenting on my performance. My mom, unfortunately, missed the excitement. She only attended home games. My father, as usual, was working, and Carla, well, her boyfriend took up her free time.

When the next year's football award banquet had come around, I knew I'd be recognized. The scene mirrored the year before. I sat amongst fellow players and their families. As coach announced the winners, I moved slowly to the edge of my seat. Time after time, he called the names of other players like Matt, who would years later become the head coach at Conyers Middle School and lead his team, which included my nephew, to the championship, something we never accomplished in our day. I watched as Matt's and other parents proudly beamed. As I flashed back to the previous year, my face tightened as tears swelled in my eyes. Before the night ended, I did hear my name. "James Brown, most valuable defensive linemen," coach said.

I leaped from my seat and shouted, "It's about time!" Grinning from ear to ear, I approached the podium. I grasped the heavy wooden plaque with both hands for fear that my mind had deceived me. Seeing my name printed in gold against the red background, I took in the moment. Afterward, I celebrated alone in my room. That night, I fell asleep with the plaque in my arms.

Soon, my happiness turned into jubilation. Rockdale County High School wanted me to play on its varsity squad. Now I knew the possibility of superstardom existed in my future. As the first eighth-grade student to play varsity high school football, I became inspired. "The Rockdale Citizen" newspaper wrote an article about me. The sports community buzzed about the prospect of another Jesse Baker coming out of Conyers. Baker lived in my neighborhood before the Houston Oilers drafted him.

Coach Sellers encouraged me to take advantage of this chance. Nervously, I walked onto the Rockdale High field and started spring training with the big boys. As we practiced, I concentrated on the drills. All of a sudden, a loud clack sounded when I tackled the running back. Coach Ron Pruitt blew his whistle and yelled, "Who was that?" There I stood, staring at the ground, standing over senior running back Timmy Smith, who lay crumpled on the field, grunting, "Oh. Oh." Coach Harbin rushed over and looked at the name taped on my helmet. "James Brown," he said before breaking into a rendition of "I Feel Good." Coach removed the tape from my helmet and said, "I can't forget your name."

I went on to become the first eighth grader to start a varsity game. However, my life still lacked something. The atmosphere at home grew both better and worse. My brother had enlisted, so I finally got my own room. Unfortunately, though, my mother stopped cooking. "You're on your own now. You grown and old enough to cook for yourself," she said. My dad got a job at General Motors, and my sister worked part time at Hardees. The family had more money, so every now and then, my mother, sister, and I would go to Avondale Mall. My mother used her Macy's card but continued to give her pre-shopping trip warning: "Don't ask for nothing 'cause we ain't got no money."

I used to ask myself, "Why we goin' then if we ain't got no money?"

My relationship with my father remained stagnant. The entire county noticed me, but he failed to acknowledge my accomplishments. Anger gripped me. By age 13, I should've been accustomed to my dad's personality, but I hadn't. In all fairness, I never expressed my feelings to my parents for fear of scorn. I couldn't fault them fully for a situation they never knew existed. My father should have known, however, that beating me and calling me "lazy ass" would hurt our relationship. I was partially to blame because I slacked when it came to cutting the grass. The rigorous workouts during practice tired me. Often, I asked my father for a reprieve, to wait until the weekend or for the sun to go down. He always denied my requests. Meanwhile, I continued to struggle to control my bowels, but outwardly I was in the best physical shape of my life. I purposely sat in the back of the classroom in case I had an accident.

These should have been the best of times, but they weren't. Somehow, I had developed expectations of how football would improve my life. These expectations remained unrealized. Both of my parents berated me, so I felt that I couldn't talk to them. More notorious than popular, I couldn't even find a girl who liked me. I doubted if anyone would care if I died. "End it all now," I said to myself. I seriously considered suicide. Football had failed at providing a reason for living. Slashing my wrists might be slow and painful. My father had a .22 caliber handgun, which he hid. I discovered it one day while I snooped in their room. Luckily, even though I had handled the gun, I didn't harm myself. Now, the gun could prove useful. Placing the trigger to my temple and pulling it would be more efficient than killing myself with a knife. At other times, I thought taking a bottle of aspirin would just be easier.

I contemplated my death for a while. Then, my uncle M.C. did something unexpected. During one of our visits, he put his arms around me and said, "I love you."

I had never heard those words before, so I asked him to repeat it. "What did you say?" Graciously, he said it again.

I heard those three words for the first time, and hearing them made me want to live. M.C. must have sensed my pain without me saying anything about my inner turmoil.

CHAPTER FOUR

HIGHS AND LOWS

That same year, I found something just as soothing as my uncle's words: "marijuana." I noticed a Ziplock bag full of the herb sitting in the door of my father's car. The pungent smell erased any doubt about the contents. Without thinking, I removed some and snuck into the house. The consequences of my dad discovering what I had done paled in comparison to the possibility of puffing on a joint. I quickly shared my discovery with my friends.

I walked three miles to the projects on West Avenue, where Nard lived. There, I met him and Burt. Though they had never shared any marijuana with me, I knew they smoked. Burt showed me how to roll my first blunt. I watched as he unrolled a cigar, emptied its contents, and filled it with marijuana. The cigar paper, Burt said, made the blunt more potent than a joint. All I know is that after I inhaled, I couldn't stop. The three of us smoked and drank our summer away. "Smoking out" is what we called the activity. We'd sit in Nard's room with the door closed and drift off into a world of temporary bliss. Malt liquor and marijuana proved to be the perfect combination. Our weed supply never dwindled much because Nard's uncles and cousins gave him whatever he wanted. My stash lasted quite awhile, but occasionally, we'd have to scrape $10 together to buy a dime bag.

With summer over, I returned to school, eager to play varsity. I wore jersey number 24, the same number as my brother. For so long, I waited to follow in his footsteps, but I wasn't able to just yet. I had to play on the junior varsity Rockdale County Bulldogs team because I missed summer training. Moving in reverse by playing on the junior team reminded me of my bench-warming days. Despite the demotion, I performed well and thought I'd be back on the varsity team soon. I failed to consider another possibility. That's why the night we played Newton County took me by surprise.

Newton County's linebacker rammed his helmet into my knee as I rushed him. The force felt like a sledgehammer struck me. I buckled and fell. Clinching the grass and dirt, I tried to lift myself. Slowly I rose, hoping to rejoin the action. But I couldn't move, and my teammates had to carry me to the sidelines. Paramedics looked at my knee and determined I should go to the emergency room. I feared the worst as I rode to Rockdale County Hospital. By the time I arrived, my knee had swollen to the size of a grapefruit. The emergency room staff gave me pain medicine and wrapped my knee. Anxiety and the throbbing in my knee made sleeping difficult. The next day, a doctor examined me and found that I had fluid in my knee as well as torn ligaments. For six to eight weeks, he estimated, I needed to cease any activity that might hurt it further. I prayed to God, who was probably surprised to hear from me, that I would heal quickly. I lost part of my mobility and relied on crutches to move about. My recuperation lasted long beyond the estimated period. Six to eight weeks may as well have been an eternity.

When the school year ended, I decided to look for a job. General Motors had recently laid off my dad and given him a severance package. With my father's new employment status and the fact that he was already tight with the family finances, I needed to make my own money. I wanted to update my wardrobe. Sears brands no longer reflected my style. I preferred Levi's 501 and Calvin Klein jeans, not Toughskins. And definitely, I would rather wear Adidas sneakers than Zips. I spoke to my father's aunt Mary Jane, who worked at Mrs. Winner's. She talked to the manager, and he hired me.

Even though I already knew a little about cooking, the first day of work overwhelmed me. I tried to remember all the information my aunt gave while she trained me to be a baker. The hot grease we used to fry chicken scared me, but because of my position, I rarely had to handle it.

Instead, I learned how to make cinnamon swirls and biscuits. My co-workers helped me feel at ease, and we always chatted as we worked. At Mrs. Winner's I met Teddy, a co-worker who would resurface later in my life. He, along with other employees, called me Pillsbury Doughboy because of my plump stomach. They even pushed my belly, imitating the Pillsbury commercials. Sometimes I wondered how the restaurant made a profit. Its employees, including myself, ate almost as much as we cooked.

I worked at Mrs. Winner's for a few months before I grew weary of depending on undependable people, especially my father, to drive me to work. I spent more time with my friends. Burt and I had a friend named McArthur Jefferson, a.k.a. Junebug. He lived two houses down the street from me. We became close when his father died in a drinking and driving accident. Because he didn't smoke or drink, Junebug helped me stay grounded. I'd spend time with him when I needed a reprieve. We'd walk two miles to J.P. Carr, the community gym, or hang out at his house. Junebug was two years older than Burt and I, so he had more liberties. He owned a car and let us tag along when he visited his girlfriend in Atlanta. He took us around the city, and at times, we'd stop to play basketball against the city boys. I welcomed the chance to play somewhere other than on Rena Court or at J.P. Carr. "Conyers" and "dull" went hand in hand. Without sports, we had nothing to look forward to.

No matter where we played basketball, Junebug always beat me at one on one. His mother let him do whatever he wanted; nevertheless, he didn't take advantage of his privileges. Watching Junebug and his mom interact was what I liked most about visiting their home. He and his mom were friends. I envied their relationship. Mrs. Jeffries spoke highly of her son. I wished my mom would do the same.

My mother, sister and I rode in a crowded rental van along with other relatives to attend Thomas' wedding. For some reason, my dad stayed home. We had never gone on a family trip before, so I relished the adventure. Everyone talked excitedly about the upcoming nuptials and Thomas' accomplishments. As we rode, I contemplated what I had to do for them to think highly of me. A short football career, however promising, could not garner the same amount of praise as attending West Point. While in Pittsburgh, I went out with Thomas and one of his friends. They bought some Red Bull. I tried it, and the taste hooked me. I brought cases of the beer back to Conyers.

Thomas and I developed a closer relationship after he joined the military. He called and spoke to me much more than he did when we shared a room. Thomas told me about West Point, Germany, and New York. Hearing his recollections inspired me. Whenever my brother came home from leave, we spent time together. Mostly, we cruised in his Chevy Chevette. Once when he came to visit, I temporarily stole his car. I wanted to drive, but I only had my learner's license. Even my mom, who recently had learned to drive, wouldn't teach me. After three tries, I would eventually pass the test, but when I saw his car in the driveway, I said, "Today is my day." While he slept, I coasted into the street.

If Thomas and I weren't cruising, we were drinking. Our trip to Savannah was one of my fondest memories. We toured Hunter Army A.F.B., played basketball, and drank our way up and down River Street. Over time, we'd both have difficulty resisting the lure of alcohol.

Eventually, my knee got stronger but not strong enough to play football by my sophomore year. To keep in shape while I recuperated and to gauge my progress, Coach Harbin asked me to play basketball. I agreed. No one knew that I actually enjoyed basketball more than football. In fact, I considered basketball my wife and football my girlfriend. A lack of confidence, however, kept me from pursuing a basketball career. Although I thought that I passed like Magic Johnson and shot like Larry Bird, football better complimented my wide 6-foot frame. Moreover, football came naturally to me and helped me release my anger. Hitting opposing players in the mouth was my signature move. I could never get away with doing that on a basketball court.

As point guard, nevertheless, I could make plays and be in control. I enjoyed distributing the ball, something I rarely did while playing football. Given that my dad had been a high school basketball star, I thought he might have a newfound interest in me, but he remained uninvolved in my sports career. No one, in fact, noticed me. When I walked on the basketball court, I became just another player rather than a star. Halfway through the season, I received a shock. Coach Harbin cut Burt and some other players from the team because of their poor grades. Athletes had to maintain a 2.0 grade point average. While I laughed and called them stupid, Coach Harbin walked over to me. They had the last laugh. My 1.67 GPA made me ineligible to play also. However, the curtain still had not closed on the GPA saga. Our varsity basketball team was stripped of the state championship title that year once officials discovered that a player who finished the season had also been academically ineligible.

Without basketball to occupy my time, I looked for another job. Burger King hired me, but I didn't work there long. I used the money I made to buy candy and sodas. I then took the snacks to school, sold them to students, and made a profit. The money helped finance my vices. Each day I could drink a case of beer easily, but I never drank at home.

I began slipping out of control. Soon, I started sneaking my sister's car before I went to school. I'd ride around the neighborhood showing off. Often I went to Nard's, where I drank Red Bull for breakfast. He had a funnel we used to guzzle the beer. Luckily, I always returned Carla's car unharmed and without being detected. Soon, though, my luck ended, and I would reap major consequences for my actions.

CHAPTER FIVE

ACTIONS AND CONSEQUENCES

Spending part of my vacation stuck in a classroom is not how I envisioned my summer. Since I failed English and history, I had no choice, however. Expectedly, my parents weren't pleased. "You want to be a stupid ass. You pay for it," my mother said. So, I paid $50 for each class.

Focusing on my schoolwork and conditioning my body became priorities. Almost daily, I trained for the upcoming season, usually by riding my bike to J.P. Carr and playing basketball. At this point, my knee could withstand the intensity of a football game, and for the most part, I could control my bowels. My body was in the best shape it had ever been.

In my junior year, coaches from across the country scouted Tom Lynch, the school's strongest overall athlete. In the process, they noticed me. The scouts spoke to us even though they weren't supposed to, and soon I started receiving letters of interest from Jackson, Oklahoma, and Grambling State universities. My coaches constantly told me that I was excelling as a player. "You can be the best football player to ever come through this small school," they said. The hype sounded good, and I believed it. In the midst of my vainglory, homework became less of a priority. Thus, I again relied on classmates to complete my assignments. Working for money became more important than working for good grades. Whenever possible I worked, bouncing between a variety of fast-food jobs.

Despite my father's unemployment, he upgraded from clunkers to newer cars. After nightfall, he'd bring televisions, bedroom sets, and other furnishings in our house. While he stockpiled material goods for himself, I, meanwhile, had to work just to buy decent clothes. Since I had trouble finding a ride to work, I could never keep a job for long. My parents looked down on me because I couldn't keep a job. Rather than focusing on my effort, they called me "sorry" or "lazy." The atmosphere at work, though, was far from discouraging. My managers considered me a good employee and appreciated my effort. Still, balancing a part-time job and practice proved difficult because the new coach, Mr. Biggs, worked us to the point of exhaustion.

Prior to one of these tiring workouts, I had an altercation with One Time. He came to my bedroom door and, as usual, wanted me to cut the grass. I asked if I could do it in the evening or on Saturday because I had practice. "You ain't going to practice, and you better get your ass out there and cut that grass," he said. I momentarily laid in the bed, obviously not moving fast enough for him. My father burst through the door and held his .22 to my head. "Your gonna do what I say, and you ain't gonna be playing no football," he yelled. "Your gonna make sure this grass is cut every week, and your gonna do what I tell you to when I tell you."

Cowering beneath his gun, I whimpered, "Okay."

Frantically, I dialed Sears, trying to reach my mom. Through tears and disbelief, I explained what happened. "What did you do?" she asked.

"Nothing," I answered. "He was fussing about that grass, and I told him I'd cut it." Our conversation lacked the reassurance I sought. In recent years, my mom had become more vocal, and my father's physical abuse towards all of us decreased. I suspect the changes were partly because our parents' ability to demand obedience purely through physical force began to diminish as we grew older and stronger. As such, I changed and became more daring. Gone were the days when I feared leaving the yard. My mom worked in the day, and my dad spent less time at home, particularly at night. So, I ventured away from home more and more. Realizing I might be too big to beat, my father used metal instead of leather to show he remained in control.

After the confrontation with my father and his pistol, I quit the team and missed the last two games of the season. Without football or the hope of playing my senior year, I became unfocused. I'm sure my mother noticed a change in my demeanor. Because I looked older, I could buy alcohol for my underage friends. At night, I came home late and typically vomited from overdrinking. I spent countless hours at Burt's. Whether or not his parents were home, we'd drink and smoke. They allowed him to drive their Cadillac, so sometimes we'd sit in the parked car listening to NWA, Too $hort, or Run DMC with the windows rolled up and lose ourselves in the smoke. Other times, we'd hang out with my cousin Kevin, M.C.'s son. He had a Chevy van we called the "party wagon." The brown, beige, and black van had all kinds of designs on it, but roominess was its most important feature. I knew plenty of guys who were eager to get high, so up to nine or 10 of us would climb into the van. Everyone put $5 to $10 together to buy gin and juice, and weed.

During spring break, my luck ended. One afternoon, I hung out with Derrick and Boo, two friends who lived on Rena Court. Like Nard, Derrick was a jokester. Boo, on the other hand, was the joke. I teased Boo and beat him up because mentally he acted slower than anyone else I knew. My cousin Darren, Mary Jane's son, also joined us. I met them at Derrick's, and on my way there, I purchased a bottle of gin. At Derrick's, we smoked, drank, played Spades, and blasted rap music for a couple of hours. Deciding I was good and high, I started to leave. I asked Derrick to place my bag, which contained marijuana, in his closet. I told him I'd come back tomorrow.

I walked home then settled into a relaxing, warm bath. Suddenly, I heard a quick knock on the door followed by my mother's voice. "James, somebody's out here to see you," she said.

"Tell them I'm taking a bath," I told her.

She knocked again, this time louder. "Somebody's out here to see you," she shrieked.

"I'm taking a bath," I repeated.

Then she burst through the door. "James, the police are out here to see you." Her wide-eyes told me trouble loomed. Despite her appearance, I had no idea why the police wanted me. I dressed hurriedly, throwing on a shirt and a pair of shorts. When I stepped outside, the whole neighborhood had gathered.

Two police officers greeted me. "You're under arrest," one of them said.

"For what?" I asked.

"Possession of less than an ounce of marijuana and giving alcohol to a minor," he answered. I held my head shamefully low as the officer pulled my arms back, handcuffed me, and led me to the backseat of the squad car. The handcuffs squeezed my wrists.

The surreal drive to Rockdale County Jail ended before I had a chance to process the evening's events. In shock, I posed for my first mug shot. The guard stripped me and made me change into an orange jumpsuit. My apprehension increased as I approached the cell. Later, I'd find out that my friends continued drinking. Boo passed out in the street. His sister called an ambulance and asked him what happened. Boo told her he was drunk and, of course, he implicated me as his supplier. His sister called the police, who after listening to Boo recount his story, searched Derrick's room. They found my bag, which had my name embroidered on it, and my wallet. With my identification in hand, the police knew exactly where to find me.

Both the temperature and atmosphere in jail were cold. About 12 men crowded the cell. Early arrivals got their choice of four beds. The rest of us lay on hard, gray mats. We shared one toilet and one shower, each covered by thin gray curtains. An assortment of smells floated around the cell. At times, I wanted to gag. Gratefully, I left the cell to hear my charges, as well as to breathe fresher air. The guards tried to shackle my ankles, but the shackles wouldn't fit. After seeing the judge, I returned to the cell, dreading the lights going out. I barely slept, frightened I'd become a victim of jailhouse violence. I glanced around the cell trying to find trouble before it found me. I looked like my father, and thankfully, some of the men recognized me. "You Tommy Brown's son?" they asked. His reputation preceded him, so I remained safe.

I spent nearly 24 hours in jail. The next afternoon, my father bailed me out. I'm not sure what upset him the most, missing time from work or seeing me in jail. One Time made me feel lower than an ant's belly with his barrage of curse words. "Where did you get that stuff from?" he asked.

Although I wanted to ask who gave him his weed, I simply said, "Off the street." The excruciating ride home made me think walking would have been more tolerable.

I sulked because my friends tattled on me. "Why didn't the police punish anyone else?" I thought. Although I knew buying alcohol for minors was illegal, Boo should've shared responsibility for his actions. To make matters worse, I came home and saw my mother's disheartened face. Her sullen eyes showed worry. At that moment, I vowed never to return to jail or to cause my mother pain.

I received 12 months of probation and a $200 fine for my actions. After the break, I found myself the talk of campus. As much as I wanted to confront gossiping students, I restrained myself. Determinedly, I set out to avoid anything that might have caused my rearrest. Nard, Burt, and others noticed a change in my demeanor. "Drugs aren't the way," became my mantra. A few months later, however, my father went to jail.

"Your daddy's locked up," my mom said. She told me the Spalding County police caught him with a couple of ounces of cocaine. Immediately, finding the marijuana in his car made sense and so did his increased spending. For a long time, I suspected that he sold drugs. On several instances, I even saw him riding around the projects. Now, I had proof.

I drove my mom almost 50 miles to the Spalding County Police Department. I sat in the car while she visited my dad. As we rode home, she didn't elaborate on their conversation or his drug dealing. My father's absence improved my mood and gave me a false sense of security. I thought I could and should be the man of the house. I applied for a minor construction job, helping to build a new Kmart. The company hired me, and I began driving my brother's Buick Regal, which he left at home while he lived in Germany. With my paycheck, I paid his car insurance and helped my mom pay the household bills. Sometimes, I ran into schoolmates who asked if I'd return to the team. I would tell them yes, but I doubted it. For a while, I experienced adulthood, but it didn't last long.

A month and a half after the arrest, my father returned home. He must have had an excellent lawyer because he only got time served. As far as I know, his case never went to trial. My father took the car from me and promised to take me to work. At first he did, but then he stopped. I sensed jail made him more paranoid. When my mom returned home from work or from running errands, he'd check the odometer and say he knew how many miles it took her to travel certain places. Sadly, I thought things would never change, so I sought comfort in old habits.

CHAPTER SIX

WOULD'VE, COULD'VE, SHOULD'VE

After my father's return, I stayed away from home whenever possible so I could avoid his unpredictable moods. With Junebug's help, Burt and I got jobs at Safehouse, where we removed asbestos shingles. Now, instead of $3.75, I made $8 an hour. Best of all, Junebug provided me with a reliable ride to work. I marveled at working with older men and hearing stories of their exploits. Easily, Greg Hamm, better known as Batman, was the most interesting. If someone dared him, he always accepted the challenge. We lived on the same street, but because of our age difference, we never socialized. I did know, however, that he used to be a star baseball player when he went to Rockdale High. Everyone expected him to go to the pros, but he didn't make it. Now, he worked alongside me, retelling stories of his glory days and his encounters with women.

Batman spoke in a high pitched voice. "You gotta work with what you got," he'd say as he rubbed his stomach and imitated his bedroom maneuvers. Everyone but me, it seemed, knew about and had experienced sex. They spoke of ménage à trois and oral sex, subjects I could only imagine. My co-workers, not my parents, provided me with sex education. I became filthy-minded and curious. After work, I drank and smoked with the Safehouse gang. In the process, I gained weight and lost focus of my dreams. Shortly before school started, I left Safehouse. Then marijuana, alcohol, and football battled for my attention.

Unprepared for what promised to be the biggest year of my life, I did everything wrong. I switched positions. God anointed me to play the linebacker position, but I wanted more exposure. Scoring touchdowns would garner attention from scouts and girls alike, I had assumed. As running back, I started playing the offensive side of the ball. With 25 extra pounds of fat, though, I ran slower. Rather than improving, my performance declined. In contrast, the team was off to a fast start and ranked in the top 10 statewide. Since we had many senior members, our fans had high expectations. At the very least, we'd be playoff bound. The Bulldogs won every home game. On the road, however, we were outmatched. Losses mounted until November when the last away game ended our playoff chances. We arrived at the stadium determined but left deflated. On the ride back to the campus that Friday evening, I looked at the solemn faces of my fellow players. "We're playing for MVP now," I commented in an effort to hype them.

The following Sunday, I borrowed Carla's car to attend the weekly team meeting. As we waited downstairs for the meeting to begin, Coach Biggs said he wanted to see certain people in his office. He called my name first. I followed him and sat down. Coach bypassed all cordialities and said, "I want you to turn in your uniform." Immediately, I asked why. "You made some comments on the bus, and we don't feel like you're giving your all," he said. "Go clean out your locker."

Blindsided, I knocked my chair over and stormed from the office. I couldn't clean my locker fast enough. I'd run through brick walls for this man and this team. I bled and sweated for them, pushing the limits of my athletic ability. I rushed to the car and sped off while I cried like a newborn. Topping speeds of 90 mph, I raced around Conyers' back roads until I got onto Interstate 20. Each curve, overpass, and cement barrier on the expressway represented an option for ending it all. I didn't know if anybody would care, but I only slowed down so I wouldn't wreck Carla's car.

As I rode, I prayed. In fact, whenever I needed something, especially before games, I'd pray. I had yet to learn, however, that God is jealous. Football proved to be the first thing I had placed before Him. I thought of my actions and how they may have contributed to my dilemma. Coach Biggs took my remark out of context. I would try to be uplifting, not sarcastic. Although I wanted to deny it, my enthusiasm did decrease after each game loss. Also, foolishly, I expected to carry my summertime misbehavior into the fall football season without consequence. Supposedly, this would be the season when I realized all my ambitions and used football as a ticket out of Conyers. During the fourth quarter of many games, though, securing a ride to McDonalds concerned me more than the final score. Until today, coach Biggs hadn't discussed my performance with me. In turn, I became complacent about the extra weight I had gained and my inability to excel as a running back when I should've asked for his guidance. Later, I found out that the coach dismissed all the African American players. Nard begged to rejoin the team, and coach conceded. I, on the other hand, refused to play for a coach who viewed me as disposable.

I tried to finish the school year without incident. However, one day, an innocent situation escalated that caused me to break my promise not to see the inside of a cell again. Unfortunately, it wouldn't be the last time. While in school, my friends and I often reenacted wrestling matches. This time, I assumed the role of announcer while Mike, Harrell, and Bobby, three of my ex-teammates, wrestled. Soon, the match turned into a fight. Shortly before lunch the next day, principal Leapold called on the loudspeaker, "James Brown, please report to the front office." Principal Leapold looked dwarfish and was rather unpopular among students. I had no idea why he wanted to speak to me. When I entered the principal's office, he gave me a 5-day suspension notice. Leapold had called my mother, but she hadn't arrived yet. He said Bobby's mother pressed charges against all the boys who wrestled with her son.

"I didn't touch him," I told Mr. Leapold.

"But you were there," he snapped.

I explained my version of the fight to my mom when she arrived, but by this time, the police had arrived. "Just go on," she told me.

I remember hearing the handcuffs snap around my wrist. Every other sound faded away. Students left their lunches to see the commotion. A year after my first arrest, I was back in Rockdale County Jail. An hour later, Mitch joined me in the same cell. "You didn't even do anything," Mitch commented.

"Yeah, I should've hit him," I said. "You're the one who hit him."

My parents bailed me out the same afternoon. This time they understood I was a victim of horseplay gone awry. My parents, the other accused boys, and I suspected prejudice prompted Bobby's mother to press charges. He was white, and we were black. Since Rockdale High barely had 50 black students, our assumption wasn't far fetched. The judge must have doubted the case's validity. He placed it on the dead docket and took no further action against any of the boys involved. Bobby transferred to Heritage High School, so I never spoke to him about what happened.

Later that year, I got arrested again. This time, the police caught me and some high school friends as we rode around a movie theatre parking lot. I don't remember the names of the guys I rode with, but I do know they had money, transportation, and offered free alcohol. For me, that's all it took. I needed something to do on another boring Conyers Saturday night. So, we chugged Bacardi 151 like it was water, endangering ourselves and unsuspecting moviegoers. The police held us until we sobered up. Thankfully, they decided not to charge us.

Before I knew it, I had graduated. When those school doors closed, I questioned what would be my next move. Having a 1.75 GPA limited my options, and procrastination prevented me from having a backup plan. I inquired about various college athletic programs but failed to complete any admissions applications. Not to mention, I skipped taking the SAT and ACT tests. Now, I doubted if I could even apply to take remedial college courses. I had placed my future on the promise of a football scholarship, and I always envisioned myself attending college. Once I got there, I'd make sure I made good grades. Without my own money, higher education now seemed beyond my grasp. So, I became like Batman: a former high school sports star with unrealized potential.

CHAPTER SEVEN

LEAVING HOME

With no clear prospects for my future, I returned to Safehouse, working as a full-time employee. I told my mother I needed a car, and she talked to my father about it. He believed in getting what you want yourself: no handouts. However, my dad did cut me a deal, offering to sell me one of the cars he repaired. "You wanna buy this car out here boy?" he asked. I jumped at the opportunity to buy the brown '84 Chevy Malibu. It had a 350 horsepower engine. Already imagining myself behind the wheel, I saved the $300 my father wanted for the car. Still, my parents kept the insurance in their name.

Though I still lived with my parents, I thought of myself as "the man." I always had fresh haircuts, wore the latest Magic Johnson and Larry Bird sneakers, and owned a car. Instead of asking my parents for money, I contributed to our family's finances. I even gave my mother money to go to the hairdresser. Since I worked on weekdays only, my weekends were free. Partying at the Night Light and other local clubs became my pastime. Erin, of all people, partied with me. She had forgiven my awful behavior.

Even after I left Conyers Middle School, I would return to the campus just to look at Erin, who was two grades below me. One of my cousins lived next door to Erin, so sometimes I would wait in my cousin's yard until Erin emerged. She treated me with the decency and respect I should've given her. Ironically, if I had treated her better from the start, I think Erin may have given me a chance. We ended up becoming true friends instead. Though my desire for a romantic relationship lingered, I gratefully accepted being just a friend.

Sometimes Erin's sister Nicole joined us when we partied. Usually, though, I went club hopping with Erin and a friend named Eric, whom we called "Hook." I met him my junior year of high school. He attended Covington High School. I related to Hook because he was a big guy like me, weighing almost 300 pounds. Hook always held a job, unlike free-loading Burt, and he had a car. Some Sundays I'd borrow Carla's car while she was at work and visit Hook. More often, he picked me up. Eric liked alcohol but not marijuana or even cigarettes. One of his friends had an apartment where we'd spend the afternoon watching football and drinking.

I went to the clubs to have fun and to meet people, especially women. I had yet to have a girlfriend. I couldn't even find dates to my high school proms. When I least expected and in an unlikely place, I found someone. Just a month after graduation, I spotted Shaundra Maddox while I watched a basketball game at J.P. Carr. At first, I noticed her tiny waist and her round derriere, which looked like a cup could sit on it. As I drew closer, I saw her smooth, chocolate skin and her straight white teeth. Expecting nothing to happen, I walked over to her and asked how she was doing. We began having a conversation, and to my astonishment, she gave me her phone number when I asked. I called the next day, expecting the person on the other end to say, "You have the wrong number." Then, I heard Shaundra's voice.

I asked Shaundra to go out with me, and she agreed. I figured I should act before she changed her mind, so I told her to get ready because I wanted to see her the same day. She gave me directions to her home, which was 20 minutes away from me. She lived with her mother in a trailer behind her grandmother's house. After I picked her up, we rode in my car and talked for about an hour. The more I looked at her, the more I wanted her. Shaundra's tight shirt and jeans showcased each curve of her body. Eventually, I mustered the nerve to tell her I had reserved a hotel room, which I actually hadn't. I asked if she'd come chill with me. She agreed, and I quickly anticipated my next move. I drove to the closest and cheapest hotel I could find, the Conyers Motor Inn. After we pulled up to the entrance, I pretended to retrieve my key from the front desk while I paid for a room. Inside, we went from talking to hugging and kissing. Then, we were naked and having sex. At 19, Shaundra was sweet but far from naïve. She already had a little girl whereas I had only imagined having sex. From the start, we both knew what would happen at the hotel. I finally had my first sexual experience, but all 45 seconds of it felt awkward. I thought we'd part ways after that fiasco; however, she came back for more.

We were together all the time after that first day. I felt like she could be *the one*. I even let my drinking buddies fade into the background. While I enjoyed having sex with Shaundra, our relationship consisted of more than that. We talked about our past and desired futures. I carefully avoided sensitive issues, such as my bowel troubles. We discussed her experience during childbirth, as well as her baby's father, who happened to be an old schoolmate of mine. Shaundra expressed her disappointment over his denial of their daughter's paternity. She respected me, especially after I told her I dreamed of attending college and playing professional football. Shaundra worked at a factory, but she said she wanted more out of life. At last, I found someone who knew nothing of my dysfunctional past. With Shaundra, I planned on making new, improved memories.

I needed a plan for our future. While watching television one day, I came across a way to take care of Shaundra and to attend college. My brother was in the Army, and my daddy had served in the Air Force, but for the first time, an Army commercial caught my attention. The announcer's voice boomed from the set. "Come in today if you want action, adventure, and a bigger challenge," he said. At the same time, pictures of soldiers in battle and performing different military jobs flashed across the screen. In the service, I'd make more money and qualify for the GI Bill. I could also secure a VA Loan to purchase a house like my father did. The next day, I drove to the recruitment office. The recruiter told me to step on the scale. At 6 feet tall and 230 pounds, I was overweight according to the Army recruiter. For my height, I had to weigh 190 pounds. The recruiter advised me to come back after I lost weight. As I left the office, I noticed a Navy sign across the hall. With nothing to lose and everything to gain, I decided to see what they could offer. The Navy recruiter said they measure body fat, not weight. Thus, he measured my neck and waist. I had a 22-inch neck and a 44-inch waist. I didn't meet the body fat requirement either. I needed to slim down to a 42-inch waist. Compared to losing 40 pounds, losing 2 inches of fat seemed easier.

The recruiter conducted a pre-interview to determine my goals. "I'm good with numbers," I said. "I want to be a disbursing clerk." He dashed my hopes after reviewing my ASVAB scores. I took the test in high school, not realizing it could determine my prospects. Throughout the test, I marked A, B, C, and D 10 times repeatedly until I reached the final question, so my score, in no way, reflected my ability. Now, I couldn't retake the test.

"You can't be that," he said.

"What else can I be?" I asked.

"A cook," he answered.

The one job I dreaded became my only option. "If I have to flip burgers to realize my dreams, then so be it," I thought. Whether for patriotic reasons, a signing bonus, or simple kindness, the recruiter worked closely with me to ensure I met enrollment conditions. The Navy paid for my visits to a spa in Athens, where I received body wraps. After wrapping my chest and stomach with plastic wrap, the therapist laid me in a steam machine. At home, I wore plastic wrap whenever possible, and I constantly exercised. For most meals, I ate salads and drank plenty of water. Every time I visited the spa, they measured my waist. Two weeks into my routine, I lost the fat. I subsequently drove to a recruiting office where I was measured again and given a comprehensive physical exam, which included a drug test. "You're going in," said the recruiter. Afterward, he swore me in.

Within a week, I'd be at the Naval Training Center in San Diego, California. Shaundra supported my decision to join the Navy and said she'd wait for me. I spent as much time as I could with her, dreading saying goodbye. My family acted nonchalant about my impending departure. In a way, I think they were happy to see me leave. The day I left, my father drove me to Harmon Airport. On the way there, we talked. During that 35-minute ride, I felt close to him. He spoke to me as a friend and a father. Sensing that flying for the first time would frighten me, he calmed my nerves by sharing his experience as an Air Force recruit going to Vietnam. Mostly, he tried to prepare me for the possibility of combat, facing death, and seeing others die. He spoke in a normal yet caring voice. To talk to my father without him cursing or fussing at me was all I ever really wanted. For the first time, I felt like he viewed me as a human being, not a nuisance. I wanted to hear more about his past and to know him as a person. As I gathered my luggage, my father drew close to me and patted my back a few times. Our partial embrace was the closest I'd ever come to hugging him. We shook hands before I walked into the terminal. With the start of my new life a few hours away, all I could think of was what I left behind. As I crossed states and timezones, I longed to be back in Conyers talking to my dad, man to man

COURAGE IN CRISES

CHAPTER EIGHT

IN THE NAVY

In March of 1990, I arrived in San Diego to begin my military career. Nothing my father had said prepared me for the reality of boot camp. Intensity filled the barracks. Rows of anxious young men lined the room — some visibly shaken, others exuding false bravado. At least 100 recruits lived in my barracks. Petty Officer Stephenson led the group. He was in his 30s, had a slender 5-foot 6-inch frame, and spoke like he was 7 feet tall. Stephenson issued uniforms, personal care items, and bunk assignments. Each recruit shared a tiny two-drawer cabinet with his bunkmate. We had to fold our clothes, socks, and underwear according to Navy specifications. Everything we owned — even our toothbrushes, toothpaste, and soap — had to be arranged neatly in those drawers. Stephenson commanded us to shower in 10 minutes or less and return to our bunks. A wall of uncovered showerheads and a wall of exposed toilets prevented privacy. Even the bathroom played a role in downplaying individuality. After showering, doctors examined us. They appeared particularly interested in our penises, which they asked us to move from side to side. I think they were checking for visible sexually transmitted diseases like crabs. For some recruits, the trip to the barbershop proved even more uncomfortable. "Stand in line and stand at attention," Stephenson barked. Hair clippers buzzed all around the room as locks of hair fell to the ground. We were becoming Navy men.

Emotionally tiring, that describes the first day. The real nightmare started at 4:30 in the morning. Deep in slumber, Stephenson's bark caused us to bolt awake. "Get up out of your beds recruits. You knuckle heads.

You asses. Pop tall recruits and stand at attention." Inspections occurred randomly. An officer would rub his white gloves over items. Finding dirt or anything untidy constituted a hit. After 50 hits, we had to do 50 push-ups and then go clean our area according to standard. If it were still unsatisfactory, a recruit would have to continue to do more push-ups and clean the area again until approved. Our beds had to be made correctly. Our haircuts had to be neat and our faces free of facial hairs. Everyone had to wear a gig line, meaning our shirt buttons were lined up with our belt buckles. If we failed inspection, we faced reprimand. Stephenson would empty our drawers, pull the sheets off our beds, and untuck our shirts. We had to do it over and do it right. That became the drill. Dropping and doing 50 pushups or having a commander's spit fly into my face while he yelled became commonplace.

The strict environment became overbearing at times. We cleaned constantly, making me think the Navy needed janitors instead of sailors. During a galley week, our chores intensified. We woke at 5:30 a.m. and then cooked and cleaned for other units. Breakfast, lunch, and dinner, we prepared it all — from soupy grits to greasy fried chicken. Military food tasted bland. My mother's so-so cooking ranked at gourmet level compared to military fare. When I worked the galley, I cooked my food and hooked it up with seasonings. That was the only benefit of galley week. In addition to the grunge work, I found my income disappointing. In the Navy, I made $150 every two weeks, a lot less than my Safehouse pay.

"What the hell have I gotten myself into?" I thought. "These folks are going to kill me, or I'm going to kill them. This is worse than living at home." I was in a different world, one that I chose this time. I quickly grew tired of Stephenson yelling in my face. I wanted to beat him down, but I couldn't. Swimming drills were especially difficult because I didn't know how to swim. The instructor told us to dive into the deep end, touch the floor, and return to the starting point. I dove in and stayed in, blowing bubbles. The instructor used a pole to grab and pull me out. A couple of days later, I started talking to the yeoman, Basil. We clicked. Basil, who processed paperwork for the captain, sympathized with me. He updated my paperwork to state that I passed the swimming test. With one hurdle behind me, I decided to become the best recruit possible and to take advantage of Navy benefits.

I went to the dentist, something I rarely did as a child. I had a bothersome, crooked front tooth that I injured after a basketball game at J.P. Carr when I was 13. I kept stealing the ball from Steve Brown, who was about 18. I must have embarrassed him because afterward, Steve ran to the bleachers, punched me, and kicked me in my mouth. I chased him, but he got away. My mother, horrified by the blood gushing from my mouth, took me to the doctor. The tooth, though still sturdy, slanted to the side. My mom and doctor decided not to remove or adjust it.

As a recruit, I couldn't leave the base. Slowly, I warmed to my environment and the men around me. I met people of other ethnicities. I had no idea Phillipinos existed before I enlisted. Also, I sought out new activities I enjoyed, for example, like cadence call. "Left, right, left," an officer would shout. I discovered my voice after one officer told me to lead a march. I gave cadence a stylistic twist. Officers and my fellow recruits complimented my creativity.

Before I finished basic training, I received unsettling news. Due to my low scores in the verbal expression section of the ASVAB, I had to leave my unit. The two weeks of training I had done wouldn't count. I packed my heavy duffel bag and walked two miles to the new barracks. As I walked, I thought of the few acquaintances I had made, mainly Basil. Starting over seemed daunting. I'd have to attend special classes with a new unit. They called the school "fast," but it was for slow students. When I arrived, I apprehensively shyed away from the group, thinking I didn't fit in. After all, I had haphazardly taken my test and could've passed it. When we marched cadence, I moved to the back of the line. Their calls put mine to shame. Regular units teased us. "There goes that fast group 2499," they'd say.

When I began speaking to the group, I learned that many of them joined for the reasons I did. They wanted to provide for their families and forge successful futures for themselves. I later realized that joining the Navy for money was backward thinking because once you serve, you are then owed. I also learned that negative behaviors I previously tried to escape, such as drug dealing and womanizing, will show up even in new places.

I met Tommie Lee Carver in fast school. Our friendship lasted well beyond basic training. Tommie Lee, a short, dark-skinned, Mississippi country boy who styled his curly hair like the singer Johnny Gill, stayed in the mirror. His anger issues rivaled mine. Fast school taught me that there's always someone tougher than you or whose life is worse than yours. In my case, Tommie Lee was that person.

I spent six weeks in fast then restarted boot camp. My unit consisted of fast students and new recruits. The newbies admired our advanced skills, not realizing the downside of our knowledge. My second basic training tour of duty lasted eight weeks, but the time passed quickly. I wrote letters to my family and to Shaundra. No one responded or attended my graduation. Nevertheless, Mess Management School, or MS, would be my next step.

Before I started school, I went home on leave. I wanted to spend those 15 days with Shaundra. I did spend a little time with my family, who treated me as if I had never left. I also visited Nard and discovered he had become a drug dealer. "You don't have to sell," I told him. "There's a different way to get out of the hood." Nard is the first nonrelative I truly loved. He loved me in return. I wanted him to live a long and purposeful life. I urged him to enlist in the Navy, and a month later he did.

I hadn't spoken to Shaundra since I left. After I arrived home, I immediately called her. My phone calls went ignored. I knew one way or another, I'd make her talk. I drove to Shaundra's trailer and literally picked her up and put her in the car. "We're going for a ride," I told her, so we went to a nearby restaurant. "Why haven't you returned my calls? So, you got somebody else now?"

"I don't want to talk about it," she said. "Why does that matter?"

Eventually, she admitted to cheating with my cousin Irvin. "He didn't tell me ya'll was kin," she said as if that lessened her disloyalty. "I feel sick. Take me home."

"No need in you feeling sick," I replied. "It's a done deal." At this point, I knew Shaundra couldn't be my girlfriend or wife. Even so, I kept having sex with her. Before I returned to San Diego, we said our final farewell.

Back on base, I excelled in MS school. The curriculum combined classroom studies with hands-on experience. I learned to measure ingredients, read and adjust recipes, and use proper cooking temperatures. My class cooked for other mess students. MS school represented a change of pace, not only from the endless cleaning but from the confinement of basic training. Now, I could make rank, move freely on base, and explore the surrounding city. I rode the trolley and even ventured to Tijuana for 50-cent beers. On weekends, I drank profusely and hung out with Tommie Lee, who was also in MS school. Like us, many on base treated drinking like a recreational sport.

I met one guy who was tired of my Atlanta nightlife stories. "We're gonna show you how it's done California style, J.B.," he said. So he and his friends took me to a warehouse. A lady wearing lingerie opened the door and asked for a $40 cover charge. I never paid that much to enter a club before and wasn't about to. My companions paid my way. The woman told us to take off our clothes and put them in a locker. We moved to the back where, as I drew closer, I saw a large group of naked men.

Thinking I was in a gay bar, I wanted to leave. They urged me to stay. Suspiciously, I peered around. We went into another room where women strolled about in lingerie, talking and shooting pool. A refrigerator sat in one corner, adding to my confusion. Then I found out I had entered a swinger's club called Thad's. About 20 rooms comprised Thad's, each containing mattresses. Sheer drapes covered the doorways, inviting voyeurism. I looked around as different scenes unfolded. The place felt imaginary, as if I had stepped into an adult movie. The club didn't sell alcohol because the possibility of sex was enough to lure patrons who, if they wanted, could bring in alcohol. Thad's exclusively catered to military couples. These men, I heard, were either impotent or wanted to see their partner with other men. If they liked you, they'd summon you to join them. One woman in her 30s approached me. Her husband, who looked to be in his late 50s, came too. I followed her into a room not knowing what to expect but eager to find out. She dropped to her knees and grabbed my penis while he watched. I kept looking back to make sure he didn't attempt to join us. When she finished, I walked about trying to become comfortable around all those naked bodies.

I used the lump sum that I received after boot camp to finance my trips to Thad's. The club helped me forgot about Shaundra, so I took advantage of the club's special, offering a free sixth day after a patron came five days in a row. Each time I brought some liquor and hooked up with the same woman. Before I had a chance to fully explore Thad's, I got my orders. I'd be stationed in Bremerton, Washington. With only three days notice, I dreaded the transition from sunny California to rainy Bremerton. I cried and drank those days away. My liver must have screamed for mercy.

In San Diego, I had easy access to Tijuana, beaches, and all the sex I could afford. My only consolation in Bremerton was that Tommie Lee would be stationed with me. This move signified the reality of being an enlisted man. I felt like the anxious eight-grader walking on the field to play with the varsity team. I packed my bags once again, focusing not on what I'd leave behind but on moving forward.

CHAPTER NINE

TURNING POINTS

I arrived in Bremerton at night and proceeded to the barge, my temporary home until the USS Karl Vincent arrived. The darkness made the barge more ominous. I had never been on any boat before, and my inability to swim increased my anxiety. "I'm a sailor now," I said to myself. The barge felt cramped and hectic, unlike the training center barracks where I had spent the last six months. I didn't even have space to hang my clothes. Each room had bunk beds with self-contained storage units, a small closet, a window, and a bathroom connected to the adjoining room. "Well, it's better than jail," I thought. At least I had my freedom, and I shared a room with an officer who made me feel particularly self-conscious.

On the barge, my days were filled with more cleaning. I became an expert in the use of bleach. Cooking even ranked higher on my list of job preferences than janitorial work. Meanwhile, I began meeting new people, including another acquaintance named Junebug, who was also from Georgia. He ranked higher than Tommie Lee and I. Junebug used his money wisely and rented a studio apartment. Despite the limited space, his place became the party spot. We'd move his bed out the way, turn the music on and up, and create a dance floor. Junebug was always jovial, and like Tommie Lee, he could be a dancing and drinking machine. But Tommie Lee and Junebug clashed, so I split my time between the two. They participated in an unending competition, especially when it came to the ladies. When I met a woman, I planned to keep her away from them both.

Bremerton was slower than Conyers. The Puget Sound Shipyard

breathed life into the blue-collar community. To get extras not provided on the barge, I traveled an hour by ferry to Seattle, Washington. When I wore my uniform, women solicited my attention, particularly on the 1st and the 15th of the month. I couldn't afford the women's company at the time, but I received a slight pay increase after ranking as an E2. Still, I needed to supplement my income. I started "slushing," or loaning money and then charging double or more for repayment. Mess school taught me that the Navy had many alcoholics who, more than often, depleted their paychecks in a few days time. Viewing their weakness as an opportunity, I borrowed $700 from a bank. I used the loan to start my business. In the civilian world, most people would've realized the absurdity of my proposition. Isolated on that barge in Bremerton, reality became skewed. Alcohol, even if only temporary, eased pain caused from loneliness, insecurity and other issues. I had experienced its power. Now, I used it to my advantage.

Once, I fought a sailor who tested my repayment policy. He avoided me at every turn. He left the galley when I entered. We bunked in the same hall, but he made himself invisible. Two paydays passed without any mention of the loan. Slushing was an underground operation, but that didn't prevent me from making a statement: pay me back or pay the consequences. We got paid on the 1st and 15th. When the 16th came, I made my move. Rooms were only accessible with keys. So, I waited down the hall for him to leave his bunk. His door opened, and I rushed toward it only to find his bunkmate leaving. "Is your roommate in?" I asked

He said, "Yes."

"Don't close the door," I said. Then, I slipped into the room, snatched my customer off his bunk, and beat him down. I got my money and reassurance that other customers now knew not to take our arrangements for granted.

The USS Karl Vincent aircraft carrier docked six months after I reached Bremerton. I stood outside to watch it come in. Its size astounded me. The barge could fit in the ship. At 19, I had never seen anything larger. It housed 5,000 men and operated like a miniature city or a floating base. Only officers got rooms. Everyone else slept in large open spaces filled with bunks. Though cramped, the barge's accommodations were nicer. At least I had a closet. Now, all I had was a trunk. Living on the ship reminded me of boot camp. The rules increased after leaving the barge, as if the USS Karl Vincent carried an air of esteem. I had to rise at a certain time, salute, and dress according to the occasion or season. For grunge work, I wore dungarees. Otherwise, I wore white dress uniforms in the summer and navy uniforms in the winter, complete with black hats and pea coats. When I ended my workday early, I still couldn't wear civilian clothes. After the ship came in, the Navy decommissioned it and put it in dry dock. The ship needed repairs.

I graduated from mopping floors to chipping paint. With a needle gun, I loosened old paint on the ship's floor until it began to peel. Then, I chipped the old paint off so new paint could be applied. I also worked fire watch. Welders came onboard and while they worked, I stood by with a fire extinguisher. Three months later, my mess hall assignment started. I regretted my eagerness to work in the kitchen. I cooked nonstop for 2,000 people. As a new crewmember, I received the least desirable assignment: grill duty. I specialized in eggs of all varieties and greasy burgers called sliders because they slid off the grill.

At the first opportunity, I moved off the ship. I met a sailor named Lamar, who looked a lot like me. He lived in military housing with his wife. They separated, she returned to Michigan, and he asked me to live with him in his four-bedroom house. We grew close within that two-month period. Lamar made me feel at ease and even welcomed my friends into his home. Nard, who was also stationed in the Washington near Canada, visited and stayed with us one weekend. I had a woman waiting for him. Despite his deep dimples and muscular build, he wasn't the most handsome fellow; nevertheless, his personality charmed the women. We partied the entire weekend. Nard got so drunk that he fell asleep and urinated in the bed.

One day I returned from work to find all of my belongings and Lamar missing. He had stolen an officer's checkbook, written bogus checks, and gone AWOL. In short, he set me up as part of his devious plan to leave. Lamar admired my jazzy style of dress, so he took all my clothes, which meant more to me than the other items. By befriending me, he decreased his expenses. I paid part of the rent and utilities, allowing him to pocket more money. Lamar's house received the brunt of my anger. I invited Tommie Lee and a large group of sailors over for the weekend. We partied; then we demolished the place. I slashed mattresses and smashed windows. I doubted if I'd cross Lamar's path again, but I hoped once the Navy located him, it would add vandalism to his list of charges. The Lamar fiasco reinforced what I already knew: People prey upon the trusting natures of others to further their own agendas. I had considered Lamar somewhat of a brother. Like with him, this wasn't the first time someone abused my trust. It wouldn't be the last.

Despite my strained family dynamic, I missed my parents and siblings. Tommie Lee substituted for them in a way. Due to his temper, however, we stopped speaking. Almost the last time we spoke was the day Tommie Lee and I caught a bus from the ferry station. A white passenger stepped on my shoe as he searched for a seat. I disregarded the action, but Tommie Lee became incensed. He despised P-knuckles, his nickname for white folks. "You better get down here and clean his shoes," he told the man. My efforts to calm him failed.

"He stepped on your shoes," he reminded me. "You need to get down here and clean his shoes, cracker," Tommie Lee said. Then he hit the man. The driver radioed the police. I had pulled Tommie Lee from the bus. No sooner than we stepped off, the police pulled up. The police spoke to the driver then approached Tommie Lee who, at this point, turned mute. I lied, telling them he didn't do anything. They politely asked me to step back, but I persisted. They called for backup and asked to see my identification. Foolishly, I continued talking without considering the consequences. Words, though, are more powerful when thoughts precede them. In my effort to protect Tommie Lee, I endangered myself. The police grabbed me, placed me on the hood of the car, and then handcuffed me. I spent the night in jail, charged with disturbing the peace while Tommie Lee went free. In the morning, I bailed myself out. Thankfully, the Navy never found out about the arrest. Following the incident, my "friend" neglected to check on me. I temporarily wrote him out of my life.

From that point on, I distanced myself from others. I ventured into the city by myself, exploring local clubs. Often on weekends, I rented a hotel room. One evening I went to the Turning Point, a happening nightspot. Routinely when I went to clubs, I posted myself near the best spot: the women's restroom. No woman goes to the club without making at least one trip there. As women walked past, I'd start a conversation. While the electric slide song played, I noticed a bowlegged young lady with a Coke bottle figure. I slid behind her. When the song ended, I asked her to dance. That one dance led to many more. As the night wound down, I asked for her phone number, and then we parted ways. Sometimes I reflect on the irony of that night. I went to the Turning Point just to have fun, but meeting that young lady led to a turning point in my life.

COURAGE IN CRISES

CHAPTER TEN

LOOKING FOR LOVE

My relationship with Tanya Jenkins almost never materialized. Over the course of the following week, I phoned her several times. We finally connected, but Tanya couldn't recall me. I asked her to come meet me, and she said okay. Tanya lived in a spacious three-story home with her parents. She caught me off guard by inquiring if I belonged to a gang. I vehemently denied her assertion. My big, buff physique and my outfit led to Tanya's perception. I wore all black, except for an Oakland Raiders jacket and hat. In Seattle, my clothing could easily be mistaken for gang attire.

Tanya introduced me to her parents. I heard her father's voice and wished I could speak like him. Her father, Willie Jenkins, or "Pape," was a preacher without a church. He had retired from the pulpit but carried the Word with him. When he spoke, people listened. Pape, who walked with a cane, strutted like a young man. He made me feel at ease, unlike his daughter. Tanya and I chatted a bit before she tried to pawn me off on her friend, Charlene, who was staying with her. I discovered Tanya was a year older than I and had a nine-month-old son, Carl. She didn't work. From what I could tell, she was a daddy's girl. Tanya's standoffish attitude disillusioned me, so I left.

The next day, I called Tanya. She told me she wanted me to meet another friend of hers, Danielle. So once again, I went to her home. Danielle and Tanya were similar yet different. Danielle, who was a year younger than I, also had a nine-month-old son and no job prospects. Unlike mean Tanya, I found Danielle easily approachable. When I looked at her, though, nothing drew me to her. I did find Tanya's older sister, Brittany, attractive. She shared Tanya's physical traits and had a welcoming personality. With Brittany, conversation flowed easily. We sat on the couch, talking and laughing. She worked as a dentist and had an 8-year-old daughter. By all accounts, Brittany would've been a better match for me, but I didn't want to start any family drama.

I instead exchanged contact information with Danielle. Later in the week, we went to the movies. She brought her son along on the date. I wondered if I could run the same game on her that I ran on Shaundra. "I've got a hotel room around the corner," I said. You want to come and chill with me?" She said "yes," so we strolled to the Seattle Inn. Inside, I rocked the baby to sleep then tried to make a move on his mother. She accepted my advances, but I couldn't perform. Perhaps nervousness prevented me from going all the way with Danielle. I had been celibate since leaving San Diego. Maybe I subconsciously thought of Tanya.

Regardless of the cause, Danielle showed understanding. "Don't worry about it," she said. "We don't have to do anything tonight." Danielle called me the next week. She wanted me to spend her birthday weekend at her apartment.

On Friday, I caught the ferry to Seattle. From the station, I called Tanya to thank her for introducing us. I told her Danielle and I went out, and I enjoyed her company. "I'm about to go over there and kick it with her this weekend," I told Tanya. Her response surprised me.

"No you're not. Stay where you're at. I'm coming to get you," she said. "You're spending the weekend with me." Like an idiot, I said okay.

Tanya drove up in her Hyundai, and then we rode to her friend Big Annette's apartment. Tilting 320 pounds, Big Annette was cool but not one to be messed with. She eyed me up and down. "You got a fine nigga. He looks nice," she told Tanya, as we sat on the couch. I tried to hug Tanya, but her body tensed, resuming her distant behavior. I wondered why she interrupted my trip to Danielle's if she had no interest in me. Tanya introduced me to Danielle; nevertheless, she interfered with our blossoming relationship. Tanya offered no explanation for her backstabbing behavior. I began playing with little Carl as I tried to deduce Tanya's motivation. Carl cooed and giggled. From the corner of my eye, I saw Tanya staring as if she had never seen a sight like this. "He don't like nobody," she said. "He don't be with no men like that."

I played with the baby a little longer before Tanya went to take him from my arms. He started crying when she reached for him, so I continued to hold Carl. Tanya told me she'd be right back and then went to the store with Big Annette. They were gone a long time. When they returned, Carl had fallen asleep in my arms. "Aah, you put him to sleep?" Tanya whispered.

"I know how to handle children," I told her. I baby sat in my early teens. My brother had a child, Deatre, before he left. Deatre's mother used to drop him off at my parents' house on her way to work. During Christmas break, I watched him. While he was with me, Deatre became my child. I rocked him in my arms, he slept in my bed, and I changed his diapers. Thomas had another son, Darrell, after he got married. Darrell's mother visited us while Thomas prepared to leave Germany and live in Hawaii. I happily rose in the mornings to feed Darrell and tend to his needs. I had always had a way with children. Someday, I hoped to have children of my own.

By the time Tanya and Big Annette returned, it was late. I almost considered myself a hostage trapped in part by my foolishness and in part by Tanya's selfishness. Rough around the edges, that described Tanya. I heard that Washington state women could hold their own and few backed down from a fight. Tanya shared that in high school she had her share of altercations. I could relate, but I didn't want to, at least not in that regard. She told me Carl's father, Carl Sr., also came from Georgia. He was an older man who worked for Boeing. While she talked, I thought to myself, "She's too mean for me. I'm a lover, no longer a fighter."

"I'm going over to Danielle's," I thought. "At least I know she'll give me some." As I drifted off to sleep, I planned my escape. When I woke up, I immediately left for Danielle's. I slept on one sofa, and Tanya slept on another.

I rose early the next morning, dressed, and quietly snuck to the phone to call Danielle. "Where you at James?" she asked. "I've been worried."

I told her I had been out, got sidetracked, and would be over shortly. Tanya blocked my departure. She looked the same but acted differently. "Come here, James. Come sit right here, she said." Then she ran her fingers through my hair and stroked my chest. She wanted to hold me. It touched Tanya to see me interact with her son.

"This is crazy," I said to myself. I told Tanya I had to leave and asked her for a ride to the ferry terminal.

"I'll do that," she said. "We gonna hook up again?"

I said "yes," but really I just wanted a ride to the station.

On the way there, I asked her to drop me off at the mall instead. I told her I'd go to the base after I left the mall. As I moved to grab my bag, Tanya slipped me a kiss, complete with tongue. I hurriedly departed, as if nothing had occurred. Inside the mall, I searched for a birthday present. I needed something to say our relationship is just beginning, but the possibility for something more definitely existed. I found a little friendship ring that cost $29.95. Now I could resume my initial plan and spend time with Danielle. I hoped she'd forgive the delay. I appreciated her wanting to spend her birthday with me. For the occasion, I wore a black, double-breasted suit, and shoes polished to a shine. I put the ring in my jacket and then caught a bus to Danielle's.

Danielle greeted me with a hug, disregarding my impoliteness. I picked up her son and began walking around with him. As we passed the window, I saw a car that looked like Tanya's. We kept walking around and then boom!

Tanya and Big Annette bounded through the door. "You a mack daddy, huh?" Tanya yelled. "I thought you were going to the base, getting on the ferry and all of that." Everyone stared at me. Mortified, I put the baby down and said I had to go to the bathroom. I tried to collect my thoughts while I listened to the unfolding conversation. "He went to the mall, so he might've gotten you something for your birthday," Tanya said.

Finally, I left the bathroom. Tanya and Big Annette had emptied and rummaged through my bag. "Ya'll didn't have to do that," I said as I hastily put my belongings back in the bag. While I bent over to pick up an item, Tanya literally kicked my butt. She was ready to fight. Carl reached for me, but Tanya quickly grabbed him.

"Don't go over there to mack daddy," she said.

I left without explaining anything to Danielle. Disheartened, I walked to the bus stop. Tanya and Big Annette rode by, shooting bullets from their eyes. Tanya initiated this situation, yet due to my foolishness, I appeared to be the culprit. When I returned to the ship, I called Tanya, but I should have called Danielle to apologize. "I'm sorry," I told Tanya.

I later learned that the three women set me up to be caught at Danielle's apartment. After I called Danielle that morning, Tanya hit redial and told Danielle that I had been at Big Annette's all night. Still, I pursued a relationship with Tanya. What a schizophrenic way to start a relationship: rejection to acceptance and then betrayal to loyalty. For a while, I couldn't predict which version of Tanya would emerge, the sweet loving one who wanted to cuddle or the vicious one whose words stung like daggers. I only knew what I felt: an irresistible urge to be with Tanya for better or for worse.

COURAGE IN CRISES

CHAPTER ELEVEN

IN TOO DEEP

After the confrontation at Danielle's, Tanya mellowed out a little. Accustomed to being around hardened men, she found me refreshingly different. We took little Carl to the waterfront and fed bread to the ducks. In fact, we would be on the go or talk on the phone regularly.

I was not only falling for Tanya and Carl, but I fell for Tanya's family as well. She had two other sisters, Candice and Rose, besides Brittany. They, along with the rest of her family, opened their homes to me. Candice entrusted me with her young, wheelchair-bound daughter, whom we called "Moo Moo." Suffering from the paralyzing side effects of a medical prescription, she couldn't speak. I often watched her while Candice ran errands. I experienced love in all the Jenkins households although Tanya sometimes acted as if she hardly cared for me. Meanwhile, I understood that she didn't want another woman to have me. Even with the mixed signals, she still gave me butterflies and caused my palms to drip with sweat each time I visited her. At least on my end, our connection felt intense, and my attraction wasn't sexual. I appreciated the way her family accepted me, especially her father. I shared a stronger bond with Pape than with my father.

I introduced Tanya's family to my navy buddies. After the introductions, Tommie Lee and Brittany began dating and so did Big Annette and a sailor named William. Every weekend we had get-togethers, usually at Rose's or Big Annette's. We'd play music and dance all night long. I made "Ready or Not" by After 7 our song. Tanya and Carl consumed my time and thoughts. I treated little Carl like a son although Tanya made a point of regularly mentioning his real father, Carl Sr., who paid child support from his hefty Boeing salary. While I caught the ferry and bus to visit his son, Carl Sr. drove a Lexus and barely came around. Although I did need a car, I refused to compete with Carl Sr., no matter how much Tanya mentioned him.

While I was trying to facilitate a somewhat stable family life with Tanya, my family back in Georgia also required my attention. Since I had enlisted, Thomas left the Army and wrecked my Malibu. My dad then convinced me to add him as a dependent so that he could help me as well as himself. My father received $496 a month. He was supposed to use some of the money to help find me another car, which I needed so that I could eliminate my reliance on public transportation and thwart Tanya's condescending comments.

One day Tanya and I quarreled because she refused to go to a local fair with me. Not only did Tanya decline the invitation, but she did so with a nasty attitude. At that point, I told her I was tired and leaving. Determined not to see her anymore, I returned to the base. I had always played the punk following our disputes even if I had done nothing wrong. I'd buy Tanya a chocolate cake — because I called her chocolate drop — or flowers and say I'm sorry. Not this time, however. I'd miss Pape the most, for I loved his tender heart. I'd also miss Sunday dinner at the table with the whole family. I felt down but determined to end our three-month relationship.

Back on the ship, I just sat on my bunk. Tommie Lee later brought me a four-page letter from Tanya. She apologized for mistreating me and wrote that she wanted to make love. Prior to this, we had only held each other and kissed. The leap from being uncaring to wanting to have sex astonished me. Apprehensively, I called Tanya and told her to pick me up from the ferry terminal in an hour. I anxiously sat, waiting for her to appear. After awhile, I called her mom. She said Tanya had already left to get me. So, I sat and sat some more until she finally came. We drove to a hotel. While I rocked Carl to sleep, Tanya showered. I recall Tanya's silhouette and glistening skin as she walked toward the bed. That pleasantly unexpected night connected us. I had always imagined her wanting me as much as I wanted her. Now, I felt like her boyfriend instead of a plaything. A week later, however, Tanya again gave me cause to doubt her loyalty.

Most people have a telltale sign that indicates when something is not quite right. A liar may be unable to keep the facts of a story straight. Someone faking happiness may wear a forced, partial smile. Rocking back and forth was Tanya's sign. As we sat in her parents' living room, Tanya clutched a pillow and rocked. "James, come here. I gotta talk to you," she said.

"What did I do now?" I asked.

She continued, "Remember the day we first made love?"

"Yes," I said, "I'll never forget that night."

She went on, "Remember I was late picking you up? Well, Carl Sr. called asking why I was keeping his son from him. We met in a hotel room so we could talk."

The more Tanya spoke, the more my disbelief increased. According to her, Carl Sr. put the baby to sleep and then started massaging her back, which led to sex. "You had sex with both of us on the same day?" I yelled. "Why did you wait until now to tell me?"

"Cause I knew you'd be mad," Tanya said, as if telling me a week later would soften the blow.

Slashing my heart with a sword would've pained me less. When I fell for Tanya, I fell deeply. Leaving her would mean leaving Carl, whom I loved as much as I loved his mother. I battled with the idea. He had learned to talk since I met them, and his first words were "James, James." However, from the moment that she admitted her sexual encounter with Carl, my trust in her dwindled. Unable to find my way out, even though she provided the perfect opportunity, I remained committed to Tanya.

In August, Carl celebrated his first birthday. Tanya had a party for him at her mother's house and invited Carl Sr. "Could you just stand back because I don't want no altercations," she said before the party began.

Astonished, I agreed. I faded into the background. Tanya's marginalization of my role made enjoying the festivities difficult. After all, Carl Sr., who lived 10 minutes away, wasn't behaving like a dad.

Little Carl recognized me as his father. I spent countless hours with him and changed his soiled diapers. The party went on, but Carl Sr. hadn't materialized. I doubted if he'd show. Obviously, Tanya sensed the same.

"Why you aren't in there with Carl while he blows out the candles?" she snapped at me. Tanya had lost her mind, but she had my heart. I acquiesced, as usual, to her latest suggestion and watched Carl blow out his candles. However, I resented Tanya because she cheated and disregarded my role in Carl's life. On one occasion, I found Tanya and Carl Sr. at Candice's house. Tanya said he had just arrived to see his son. I sensed her explanation was suspicious, but like always, I stayed with her.

Like with Tanya, I perhaps trusted my father too much. I figured he should've saved enough from the dependent money he received each month to buy me a car. I called home, and Carla told me he recently purchased a stylish, black Nissan Maxima. I spoke to my father about our arrangement. I wanted the Maxima because riding the bus and ferry inconvenienced me. "I ain't got no car for you to come get," my father said nonchalantly. I only added him as a dependant at his suggestion during a time when I was heartbroken and homesick. I felt he deceived and used me. At the very least, I knew my dad could've repaired a used car for me. Now, he upgraded his ride while I rode public transportation.

Although I had Tanya's family, at times I still felt isolated and alone. Seeing Tanya and her ex-boyfriend together dealt a blow to my ego and sense of security. "This relationship isn't going to work," I thought, "and my dad's tripping." I went back to the ferry terminal. While I sat, I pondered, "If I get back on this ship, I know I won't see Tanya again." So, I called her crying. In between sobs, I said, "My daddy's dead. Come get me." Of course, my father was alive, but I told her he died from a heart attack, which he later would. Both my father and Tanya had stomped all over my feelings, but I chose to mentally and emotionally bury the lesser of two evils.

Tanya took me to her home. Her family gathered around me, providing comforting words. Tanya wiped my heavily flowing tears. As each tear rolled down my face, I released stress. I called Junebug in Conyers, told him what happened, and asked him to call the Navy chaplin to in-form him of my dad's "death." The military granted me a 15-day leave, so I returned to Conyers.

Again, I spoke to my father about getting the Maxima or any car; again, he denied me. Three days later, the Jenkins' sent condolence flowers to my parents' home. "What the hell is wrong with you?" my mother asked. "You telling people your father is dead?" No words could explain my actions. I retreated to my room and closed the door. No one told my father what I had done. Still livid with him, I basically ignored him. I returned to Seattle and spent the last five days of leave at Tanya's house.

Three months later, Tanya suggested that we move in together. She wanted to leave her parents' home and be independent. Besides, she said, "Take your hoes to the hotel, not me." Tanya refused to go back to a hotel. A room at the Marriott averaged about $100 a night, and I subsidized our stays. Easily, I could afford a small apartment, so I agreed.

Her father said, "I'm trusting you with my baby. All I ask is that you don't hit her. I ask that you take care of her because I trust you." I assured Pape I'd do right by Tanya, and that was my intention. We rented an apartment in Renton, 20 minutes outside of Seattle.

When we moved, our fights escalated. Previously, I bowed to Tanya's wishes when we had disputes. Giving in dissipated our disagreements and allowed me to avoid following in my parents' abusive footsteps. Now that we were on our own, words often evolved into blows. Nothing should have led to hitting Tanya, but she incited me and threw the first punches. Eventually, I hit back. Over time, Tanya developed a conscience, and our living together, or "shacking up," became inappropriate. She also complained because I wanted to have sex frequently. My suspicions began to rise, so I asked if she wanted me to stay on the base. After all, we got the apartment in part for more privacy.

My every action seemed to provoke her irritation, and I couldn't compensate, especially in comparison to Carl Sr. I'm not sure if Tanya compared me with the baby's father to get a rise out of me or she genuinely liked him better. She compared our lovemaking by saying Carl performed certain sexual acts better than I. She also looked down on my meager military pay. "If little Carl needs something," she said, "all I got to do is call his daddy."

"Where was his daddy?" I thought. He certainly wasn't at his birthday party. When Carl woke up each morning, he called for me. I provided for Tanya and Carl to the best of my ability. I told her that I wasn't rolling in money, but as time passed and I advanced in my military career, my income would increase.

Tanya and I were young and inexperienced in the realm of mature, healthy adult relationships. Living together exposed and magnified our good and bad qualities. On one rainy night, I grew weary of arguing. Consequently, I packed a sea bag and left for the ship. I stopped onto a street corner, waiting for a green light. As I crossed near the ferry terminal, I felt something hard pressing at my side and then a jolt of force. Seconds later, my body hit the cold, wet pavement. Darkness enveloped me.

CHAPTER TWELVE

RETURNING HOME

Without regard for my safety, an automobile driver struck me and left me in the street. I awoke briefly as the paramedics cut my goose down jacket and positioned a brace around my neck. When I regained consciousness, I was laying in a hospital bed. To ease the throbbing in my back, the doctor prescribed pain medicine. Temporarily paralyzed, I couldn't move. God sometimes shows a sign of things to come.

After a few hours, my mobility returned. The doctor discharged me and ordered three days of bed rest. I informed him of my military status. He assured me he'd report the incident to the ship's physician. I returned to the apartment and told Tanya what had happened. Over the next three days, Tanya's actions led me to further question her commitment. Despite our previous argument, I expected her to take care of me. Thinking back, I shouldn't have been surprised.

I needed her then more than ever. The warm, caring woman who comforted me after my father's "death" showed her thoughtlessness now. I asked Tanya to do simple things, such as cooking canned soup. She refused. I stumbled around, wincing from the pain. To ease my discomfort, I borrowed one of Pape's canes.

I guess my injury interrupted Tanya's cozy routine. Tanya had grown accustomed to sleeping until noon. Before I went to work each morning, I'd bathe Carl and put him back in bed with her. When I came home from work, I'd play with Carl or take him on walks around the apartment complex. I did the things with him my father never did with me, so I tried to show Carl how much he meant to me. Though he could barely verbalize his feelings, I knew Carl loved me. I felt it.

I returned to the base four days after the accident. It was in the evening on Halloween weekend. I went to the clinic and signed in. I told the coremen I had severe back pain. They said they were about to leave for the weekend. Perplexed, I asked if anyone was able to examine me. "No," they said. "Report back on Monday." The Navy wanted me to protect and serve but examining my injury ranked low on its list of priorities. Fed up, I returned home and stayed there for over two months. Tanya asked why I was home every day. I lied by telling her the doctor ordered me to take time off.

I spent a lot of time with Pape and Carl while I recuperated. Usually though, I sat at home and tried to move as little as possible. My lower back felt like someone hit me with a hammer. Then, even sex lacked enjoyment. I lived off my diminishing savings. Tanya thought I was receiving my normal income, though. I used some of my savings to buy Christmas gifts for Tanya and Carl.

I anticipated spending the holiday with the Jenkins. Tanya's family opened gifts at midnight. In the late afternoon, they gathered for a festive dinner. I longed to be an official member of her family. I asked Pape for his blessing, which he granted. On Christmas morning, I proposed to Tanya. "Treat her right. I love you like a son," Pape said as he gave me his approval.

Nervously, I shopped for an engagement ring. Tanya would scoff at a cluster ring or one that didn't sparkle just right. I enlisted a saleslady's assistance. "I need a ring that will make her say damn!" I told the saleslady. "Something she can't say no to." She showed me a gold, solitaire engagement ring that linked to a matching wedding band. When I saw the set, I imagined it on Tanya's finger. I knew she'd adore it. I placed the ring in a necklace case, put the case in a shoebox, and put the shoebox in a big box stuffed with paper. Tanya would have difficulty determining the contents of the present, and that was my plan.

When Christmas morning arrived, I watched Tanya struggle with the boxes. "What's all this?" she said. I snuck down to the basement to retrieve a hidden surprise. While Tanya fumbled with her gift, I quietly slid next to her on bended knee. I handed Tanya a chocolate cake frosted in her favorite colors. "Will you marry me?" was written on top. Tanya cried and gave a theatrical performance as she accepted my proposal. Everyone asked when the wedding would occur. We decided to marry in the spring of 1992.

By January, my back pain had decreased. Tanya and I both needed an evening to ourselves, so I decided to go to a club. Tanya, whom I'm sure felt a little smothered, willingly lent me her Hyundai. She wanted me out of the apartment as much as I wanted to get out. I knew I couldn't dance with another woman at the club, but I could mingle. I planned to stand near the women's bathroom, my usual spot, and simply talk. As I made a turn in the club's parking lot, a sharp pain surged through my back. I momentarily lost control and scrapped against another car.

Security guards witnessed the incident. "Uh oh," I thought. "Let me get the heck out of here." I sped off, only to be stopped by the police moments later. They ran my identification and discovered my AWOL status. I had blasted Lamar's cowardly actions. Now, I found myself in a similar predicament. The police took me to King County Jail in Seattle. Shortly afterward, Naval police arrived. Their show of force was unnecessary. They came in a three-car caravan as if I had committed espionage. Each black car had tinted windows. The Naval police wore their dress blues. Four men rode in the car with me, two in the front seat and one on each side of me in the back. They transported me to the brig.

Immediately, the police made me undress. Leaving nothing to chance, they searched every inch of my body's surface and within each cavity. The officers noticed my hobbling. As a result, they placed me in solitary confinement. The police notified my family. They were concerned about my physical condition after the accident, but as long as I was alive, my incarceration was no big issue.

Unless I had a visitor, I rarely left the cell, even for meals. The kitchen staff delivered my food and slid a tray through a window in the door. Tanya and I had been engaged only two weeks before my arrest. I wasn't sure if she'd support or desert me. She came to see me each week. During those visits, we had to keep our hands on top of the table. Every now and then, the guards let us hug and kiss goodbye. My love for Tanya increased though I still mistrusted her. She showed genuine concern about my well-being. Pape even came once. He could not bear to see me locked up, so he didn't return.

Thirty days after my arrest, a Navy lawyer visited. The lieutenant representing me said he'd secure my release without me having to serve additional time. The clinic log proved I had sought medical treatment. However, the base refused to accept me back. The lieutenant sympathized with my situation. "People have done far worse than this," he said. He presented two choices: go before the captain for a hearing or take an other-than-honorable discharge.

"How long will it take for me to see the captain?" I asked. He was unable to guarantee when I'd have a hearing, and I refused to sit behind bars for months on end. "How long will it be if I take the discharge?" I asked. He said it would take a week to process.

Without fully thinking about the impact of my decision, I selected the quickest option. Disillusioned with the Navy, I sought a change, something more exciting than cooking. Moreover, I no longer wanted to follow the Navy's rules. Before the hit-and-run, I had been a good sailor though my efforts went unrecognized. Surely, in the private sector I could make more money. I also wanted to reunite with Tanya as quickly as possible. One swift signature ended my two-year enlistment. In order to maintain a responsible image, I pretended to have an honorable discharge, complete with benefits.

I relished my renewed freedom — no more grilling those greasy sliders or wearing a uniform. At the time, I failed to realize that the Navy's rules served a purpose. I underestimated the value of discipline.

Post-military job prospects were few and far between. By April, I had depleted my savings. Tanya's child support and food stamps sustained us. Broke, busted and disgusted, I sought assistance from an unlikely source: my father. I called him. "I'm here in Seattle without a job or money," I said. "The Navy kicked me out. Can you help me?"

"I can show you how to make some money, boy," my father answered. He sent a one-way plane ticket. Before leaving, I discussed my plans with Tanya.

"Do what you want to do. Your gonna do it anyway," she snapped. I told her I would send money for her and Carl. I told her that I had gotten my military benefits and that I was going home to get a place for us to live.

My father didn't disclose how he'd help me make money, but I had an idea. When I returned home, he revealed his money making machine.

CHAPTER THIRTEEN

LIKE FATHER, LIKE SON

Since my father's layoff from General Motors, I had been curious about his vocation. His arrest exposed his profession, but no one in my family dared speak the truth. Several times before leaving Seattle, I watched the movie "New Jack City." I wanted to delve into the drug culture, a world where my father had now submerged himself. Watching the movie's main character, Nino Brown, solidified my view that no good could come out of dealing. Still, I understood how selling drugs could entice even the strong-willed.

Shortly after I arrived home, my dad called me into the kitchen. We were alone except for my 7-month-old nephew, Roderick. My father methodically moved about in the kitchen as if he were cooking a meal. In a way, he was. Crack put food on his table.

I watched as my father boiled water then stirred in cocaine and baking soda. This process, he said, decreased the cocaine's strength while increasing the quantity of crack. For a tangy twist, he added Orajelâ. After we made the first batch, my dad put the crack on a plate where he divided it into small pieces using a razor blade. My father weighed the crack rocks on a scale and then followed that with a quick accounting lesson. "These are dimes, which are $10," he said. "These are twenties, or you can sell slabs for $100 or eight-balls for $125." Dimes were as small as a single piece of Nerdsâ candy. An eight-ball was no larger than an Oreoâ cookie. Back then, ounces sold for $1,500, which wise dealers could cut up and sell for $4,000.

The financial potential lured me, and the entire process seemed too simple. As with most deceivingly easy endeavors, there was a catch. In time, I would discover the real cost of fast money. My father started me off with a $100 slab because I could double my money and repay him.

"What was it about this drug that caused people to lose their minds," I wondered. Despite the size of the rock, addicts lived for and killed over crack. In the '80s, marijuana was a popular drug of choice. By the early '90s, crack cocaine had a vice-like grip on many African American communities. Rockdale County was no exception.

Crack caused Conyers and nearby suburbs to change. Once welcoming neighborhoods now resembled ghettos. Freshly painted houses looked out of place. Trash littered streets and immobile cars sat in driveways. Men loitered on corners long past nightfall. Everybody appeared to be selling or using. In fact, finding anyone who wasn't doing either was difficult. Even Junebug had begun slinging. My father's good friend who routinely helped him repair cars started doing crack. Now a crackhead, he'd install an engine for crack. Former schoolmates and older adults whom I had once admired were cracked out and transformed into zombies. People who were once good workers lost their jobs when they failed drug tests. Men and women who used to have curvaceous, toned figures became thin as a rail. Crack lined the pockets of its dealers and stole the souls of its users. The drug claimed both of my brothers. Yes, I had two brothers.

Six months before I left for the Navy, I discovered my father had other children. They lived 10 minutes away. I learned of my illegitimate siblings from talk on the street. "Your daddy's got a son," I'd hear people say. With the help of Dwayne, one of my brother's friends, I went to investigate. He knew of a teenager who claimed to be my father's son. Dwayne drove me to Covington, where I met Frank. He looked nothing like my father or any of my relatives. Frank was a quiet, shy 15-year-old. He had a twin, Frieda, and two younger sisters. I met everyone, including his mom.

Awkwardly, I tried to be a big brother to Frank. I spoke to him about school and his failing grades. Our relationship had just begun to blossom before I returned to the Navy. He met Erin, my former love, and they began dating. Sometimes, I'd take her to see him. When I came home on leave a couple of times, I brought him some clothes.

When I asked my dad about his other children, he bluntly said the kids were his. I kept his acknowledgement to myself. Still, the rest of my immediate family eventually found out. My mother never accepted Frank and his siblings, however. According to her, only a DNA test could validate their paternity.

By the time I returned home from the Navy, Frank had perfected the role of the stereotypical drug dealer. I watched incredulously as my once timid brother smoked weed, drank, and made more money than men twice his age. Frank's new-found lifestyle superseded graduating from high school. He dropped out and rode around in a supped up Cadillac. He had money and flaunted it. Frank dressed stylishly and women flocked to him. Money from selling drugs gave him confidence. Frank, along with other dealers, ran a fast-food style drug operation. An endless stream of addicts drove up, bought dope, and drove off. Police patrolled the area but not to curb drug use. They'd wave and keep going.

In contrast, crack did nothing to improve Thomas' life. He left the Army and divorced his wife, but I can't say if his drug use started before or after either event. I do, however, know that he ultimately lost the ambition that garnered his acceptance into West Point. I once admired his drive and looming success, but now he worked as a convenience store stock clerk, a job with few possibilities for advancement. With limited options and means, Thomas stole to support his habit. His thievery extended to our household. He looked the same but acted and smelled different. A musty odor clung to him. I saw the effects of drugs on my brothers, and I still chose to join the game.

After my father showed me how to make crack, he drove me around Conyers and nearby Covington. We rode to various locations and neighborhoods. He showed me who to sell to and who to avoid, pointing out loyal customers and probable cops. Selectively choosing his clients and selling spots had been the keys to my father's success. With his help, I'd become the Robin to his Batman. Together we'd control a major share of the drug game. He'd work one side of town while I worked the other.

My father treated drug dealing like a large, brick and mortar enterprise. He ran the operation mainly from the back room of a small Conyers apartment. He had a group of cracked-out employees who served as couriers, scouting out customers. My dad's employees would collect money from buyers, bring the money to my dad, and deliver the crack to the customers. My dad paid his workers in drugs, throwing them a dime bag every now and then. With the exception of me, he never sold to other dealers, and he never revealed his supplier.

My father and I finally bonded over eight-balls and dime bags. He sold me a Cutlass and set me up with a few clients. Whenever my clients craved a hit, they paged me. If my father's clients couldn't find him, they would contact me. I even began selling other controlled substances from the trunk of my mobile storefront. I sold beer, liquor, and occasionally marijuana. On Sundays, I actually benefited from the Georgia code that prohibited alcohol sales. I was able to pad my pockets and lifestyle because junkies exchanged items that were worth much more than the amount of crack I supplied. They bartered clothes, VCRs, TVs, jewelry, and other valuable items for crack.

Ironically, Nard led the life I left behind, and I took on the life he had left behind. While I learned the ins and outs of dealing, he continued and eventually completed his Naval enlistment. I had convinced him to lead a life without drugs and seek a future in the military. Later, we'd discuss the hypocrisy of my role reversal.

I intended on staying in Georgia for a short time, just long enough to save for my future. I wanted to pay for the wedding, prepay the apartment rent for about six months, and be able to look for a job without worrying about money. I had good intentions, but even the best laid plans come undone.

CHAPTER FOURTEEN

UNDER THE BIG TOP

I sometimes wondered if there would ever be enough dealers to feed the insatiable desire for crack. My business increased to the point that people said I had become the real Nino Brown, no longer Robin. Addicts in Conyers knew me as J.B. If my father ran out of his supply, I'd buy from a guy named Steve, who was a friend of Frank's cousin. I don't know what he used in his batches, but he had the secret recipe. Once I began selling his stuff, my pager beeped continuously. Junkies were ready to trade anything and everything.

As business boomed, I put my money in a shoebox under my bed or in my car trunk instead of investing or saving my money. I hid my earnings and drugs from Thomas because I knew he'd steal them. One day I came home to find him screaming at his girlfriend. No words could calm him, so we began fighting. I drew my pistol. Our mother began hollering, "Ya'll don't be acting like that."

Shortly afterward, Thomas moved to St. Louis with his girlfriend. She had no idea he used crack. While I denounced Thomas' change in demeanor, I contributed to it since I sold him crack. In my feverish pursuit of money, I had abandoned my morals and aided in my brother's deterioration.

Word spread that J.B. had the good stuff, and it also helped that I delivered. People believed I ran a big-time operation and sold kilos. Dealers even started buying from me. Like a savvy businessman, I sold to them so I could turn a profit faster. I never gave away freebies, but I did share the perks of my business with old friends. Some women, as my father taught me, traded sex for crack. We called them tricks. When a trick wanted to strike a deal, I'd take her to Junebug's apartment. I rarely had sex with these women, for Tanya still had my heart. The times I did cheat were justified, I felt, because she had cheated on me. For all I knew, she could've run to Carl Sr. as soon I left. Normally, I passed the women off to Junebug or Burt. Between the two of them, I knew I'd find a taker. My friends paid a discounted rate to the women who, in turn, paid me and received their crack.

I took my business seriously. As in my Navy days, I occasionally found it necessary to make an example out of a customer. Robin was a regular trick. One day, I gave her some dope prior to receiving payment. Robin said she didn't have any money, so I dropped her off at the apartment so she could do what she had to do to pay me. "You better go up there and make you some money," I said. I waited and waited for her to come back. At last she appeared but without my money. Robin crossed me at a terrible time. I was lit from an alcohol-induced buzz. "Your about to ride with me," I told her. I threw Robin in my trunk, raced out of the parking lot, and took her for a ride. I had to make sure she got it right: Think twice before swindling me. Robin pounded on the trunk while I drove up and down I-20. "You don't like that?" I yelled. "I want my money now." Our adventure lasted about an hour. She got the message.

Like Frank, I flaunted my success. Everybody wanted J.B, and I put on a show. Going from making only $300 on the 1st and 15th to $5,000 over the course of a weekend inflated my ego. I carried wads of cash. "I have enough money to choke a cow," I'd say as I waved the money around. I ate out constantly. Steaks were a staple in my diet although I did savor fried chicken. I would eat an eight-piece chicken dinner all by myself. Due to my chronic back pain, I rarely exercised, so I packed on the pounds. I bought things I always wanted, including attention. I sported more gold than Mr. T and had more shoes than one man needed. I wore a different designer outfit on each day of the month.

I was a hot commodity. No longer the invisible man, women found me irresistible. Some were acquaintances who looked right through me in the past. One woman, Sonya, simply wanted to be seen with me. She was six years my senior. I sometimes let her tag along as I conducted my business. Having a woman with me, for some reason, attracted more customers. Sonya provided interesting conversation, and at times, she'd drive me around because the Cutlass had mechanical problems. Also, my father harped about it having high mileage. Instead of buying a new car, I rented one for $9.99 a day. Each week I drove a different car.

Of all the women I met, Sonya seemed the most sincere. We had a platonic friendship. Even with her sitting next to me, ladies approached my car and made sure I noticed their lack of underwear. When I partied at clubs, I ordered champagne and drinks for friends and strangers. Women flirted everywhere I went, but at this point, I still only wanted Tanya.

By July, I longed for Tanya, so I flew her in for a week. I brought her to a hotel where surprises waited: a cake and two beds covered with clothes. The cake read, "I miss you." The clothes reflected her hoochie-momma style. I bought her tight fitting dresses and cheetah print outfits to add to her collection.

During her stay, we enjoyed each other and the city. We visited Six Flags, Atlanta's Underground, and other downtown spots, making purchases at jewelry stores along the way. We also went clubbing. Tanya liked Atlanta's vibe. She had never seen so many blacks who owned businesses and were doing well. I had no problem splurging on Tanya, but being apart from her helped me develop a backbone. Previously, I would've walked through a fire with gasoline drawers on for her. I sensed now, however, that Tanya loved me more than I loved her.

I took Tanya to Sears to meet my mother. Since I had lied about my father's passing, I avoided my parents' home. Carla came by the hotel, and they clicked. My mom and sister nicknamed Tanya "Black Pearl."

"James loves his Black Pearl," they told her. Tanya failed to question my income supply. Though I told her I had received medical payments from the Navy, my spending spree should've raised suspicions. I reassured Tanya before she departed for Seattle that the only reason that I left her was because I needed to make some money for us in Georgia. If my settlement had been enough to live on, I explained, I would have had no need to leave at all.

Tanya called me when she reached home and said that she wanted to live in Atlanta. We decided that after the wedding in Seattle, she'd move. Prior to leaving Seattle, I had prepared myself for the possibility that the distance might end our engagement, but surprisingly it hadn't. Gerald Levert's "Baby Hold on to Me" was our new song, and I definitely wanted to hold on to Tanya. I feared my lies would tear us apart, however.

Once Tanya left, the reality of our future became unavoidable. Tanya and her bridesmaids had already been fitted for their dresses. On the other hand, I had done little planning for the big day. The guys from the boat were out to sea, and I had lost contact with them after my release from the brig. I had no groomsmen. There was one sailor, Bruce, whom I wanted to sing. He worked in the communications field, so I could call him. I procrastinated, and now his participation hadn't been confirmed. I panicked and slipped into extreme selling mode because I had to pay for the wedding and a place for us to live. I had put aside roughly $5,000. I could've and should've saved more, but the more money I made, the more I spent.

Without hesitation, I sold to any and everyone. Sometimes, a few of my father's premium customers stopped by the house. If he weren't home, I'd deal to them. I also had customers stopping by. Needless to say, my actions angered my father. We had small arguments until he exploded. "Don't have people coming over here!" he yelled. "Don't be selling at the house." I left the house and stayed at Junebug's for a few days. Then I rented a room at the Conyers Motor Inn. When I grew tired of spending money on the hotel room and thought my dad had calmed down, I went back to home.

My father often expressed concern that I was doing too much too fast. Mostly, I dismissed his comments as jealousy. My father wore a string necklace that had a small shell containing garlic hanging from its center. He believed the necklace shrouded his dealings and kept him beyond law enforcement's radar. I questioned the necklace's power, but I should have heeded my father's instincts.

CHAPTER FIFTEEN

BEGINNING OF THE END

The countdown clock ticked on my September nuptials. Dealing drugs had to end at some point. With Tanya and I moving in together again, I knew she'd become suspicious. Besides, I did not want my current lifestyle to become my legacy. So, I sought to maximize the time I had left, selling day and night. When customers called, I quickly answered. One evening I ran into Teddy, an old acquaintance, from Mrs. Winner's. He wanted dope but had no money. What he had, however, was a new, fluorescent orange beeper. Not one to give away anything, I traded a twenty bag for the pager and nonchalantly moved on to the next customer.

I had product to sell and money to make. In my mind, I had placed myself in a desperate situation. I had less than two months to prepare for the arrival of my ready-made family who included the woman I loved and her son whom I loved like my own. I also had secrets hanging over my head that, if exposed, might have caused me to lose everything. Despite my drive for money, I wasn't callous towards people who didn't fit into my financial equation. As I rode around one afternoon, I saw the younger sister of a former classmate. Shaneka walked as if she carried a tremendous burden. I drove closer and noticed the 15-year-old's protruding stomach. "What's that, girl?" I said.

"Don't start. I have to hear about that from my momma," Shaneka answered. "Ain't nobody trying to help me."

My heart went out to her, so I asked what she needed help with.

"You see I'm walking," she said. "I need rides to my doctor's appointments." I told her to call when and if she needed anything.

Prior to her next doctor's visit, she called me for a ride, and in time, I think she developed a crush on me. Small-town chatter started. People wrongly assumed we had a sexual relationship. I extended my assistance to Shaneka because I knew how it felt to lack options and feel alone. Now busybodies were making other insinuations.

All the while, Teddy fixated on the pager he gave me. The old Teddy I worked with would've accepted the loss. After all, I didn't steal it from him. Crackhead Teddy lacked the capacity to focus on anything other than the next high. I ran into him again, but this time at a stop sign in front of his house. Teddy stood outside with one of his younger male cousins. Before I knew it, they rushed to my car. Teddy came to the passenger side. His cousin stood at the driver's side door. "Man, you got that pager?" Teddy asked.

"What pager?" I responded.

"You know, the one I told you to hold," he said.

"Man, you ain't told me to hold nothing. I gave you what you wanted, and it's over with," I told him.

"That's my girl's pager," Teddy said.

"Sorry," I answered, "it's over with."

Suddenly, his cousin sucker punched me in the face, and I sped off. The next day I saw Teddy's scoundrel of a cousin at J.P. Carr gym. Other than us, the gym appeared empty. I charged after the boy, but he outran me. He sought haven in the coach's office. Realizing the coach was working, I left. Later, I found out that the punk had called Teddy and some more of his cousins. They came back to J.P. Carr searching for me. Ultimately, what started as a business transaction escalated.

Teddy's girlfriend came to my house demanding the pager. I let her in the house. Initially, I spoke nicely though I did lie. I told her I had lost the pager. She still wanted it. I became brazen. "These fools must not know who they're messing with," I thought. At 300 pounds, I had a 24-inch neck, which was bigger than many women's waistlines. I feared no one, especially females. "You ain't getting it back, so you might as well leave," I told his girlfriend. "Go talk to your man about the pager." She left, but Teddy still didn't let the incident go.

Without knowing it, I had placed a target on myself. Teddy's inability to afford a twenty-bag showed his financial instability. Still, he faulted me not only for the pager's loss, but also for the belittlement of his girlfriend. He sought to settle the score by sending a Trojan horse my way.

I met Lionel Lee, an up-and-coming dealer, or so I thought. He was a brawny Texan who looked like he quite possibly belonged to a gang or a band of wild gorillas. He bought a $100 slab and then an eight-ball. Almost everyday he called or paged me, requesting more drugs. "His business must be thriving," I thought. One night, Sonya and I met Lionel in the parking lot of a hotel. I immediately noticed in the passenger seat Teddy's young cousin, the one who punched me. Seeing them together aroused my curiosity. I learned that Lionel was Teddy's cousin and the uncle of the pregnant girl I had befriended. The rumor mill, churned by Teddy, had obviously gotten Lionel's attention. Still, I ignored the obvious because Lionel had gained my trust.

By the time Lionel came into the mix, I had reached the height of my career. I worked hard and lived harder. Gambling and drinking helped relieve my stress. One night I gathered with some high school friends to play Tonk. With each card game, my losses mounted until they reached nearly $500. In spite of my losing streak, I wanted to continue but suggested we play for dope. My opponent refused. "What, you ain't got no money?" he taunted. I snatched his winnings from his hand and ran. An angry crowd chased me. I tried to reach my trunk, where I hid a gun. All my good eating and hard drinking caught up with me because my overweight physique hampered my escape.

Before I made it to the car, I felt bodies colliding with mine. As the fight ensued, someone yelled, "Call the police." They arrived shortly thereafter. I tried to discard the dope and threw some of it under my car. Snitches in the crowd told the police what I had done. To stop them from searching me, I faked an injury. My back did hurt, but not to the point where I needed medical attention. "It's not my dope," I told the police between my labored breaths. The ambulance came and the paramedics laid me on the stretcher. I hoped the noise and confusion caused by the intoxicated crowd would work to my advantage. I slipped the rest of my drugs to

Burt. Someone unfortunately noticed the exchange. Burt took off running, but the police caught him and brought him back to the squad car. Idiotically, I left the stretcher and volunteered to go to the precinct. From that point on, my mouth got me into trouble.

Anyone who has seen a cop television show knows the mantra: "You have the right to remain silent." Not only did I give up that right, but I also spoke without requesting an attorney. I sat in the interrogation room and basically did the detective's job for him. "I ain't selling. I'm a user," I blurted out. With more than 100 bags of crack in my possession, I hoped pretending to be an addict would save me from years of incarceration. The detective said I had been booked for possessing cocaine with the intent to distribute. All of the tiny, resealable plastic drug bags had my fingerprints on them. I faced five to ten years in jail.

"What do I have to do to get out of here?" I asked.

"Wanna give us some names?" the detective said.

I told him I wanted to talk. He then brought in another detective.

The second detective promised to release me in exchange for another dealer. He told me I'd have to set up someone. I asked who, and his reply stunned me. The police wanted my father. They considered him an elusive, yet major player. My arrest presented an opportunity for them to finally catch him. I played crazy. "Give me somebody else," I suggested as if I had other options. "I don't know what you're talking about. My daddy ain't selling."

The detectives persisted, but I never wavered in my denials. They named other dealers, including Steve, my supplier. I pretended not to recognize his name. Next, the detectives talked about Michael Harris. "You get Harris," one of the detectives said. "He makes my dick hard."

I had bought from Michael before. The police needed to arrest him with 3 ounces so he'd serve federal prison time. From my time in the brig, I knew the police used informants who were eager to reduce their jail sentences to nab other suspects. I agreed to the deal.

The next afternoon, the detective elaborated on the plan. I'd receive money to buy small increments of cocaine, starting with a half ounce. The police would wire me and videotape each transaction. Once Harris sold me 3 ounces, I'd be a free man. They'd relocate me and give me a new identity. After two years, they said, I could leave the witness protection program and return to Georgia. Within that time span, they assured me people would've forgotten about me.

The police recorded our conversation. Again, I said I wanted to go home. The police let me set my bond. I told them I could afford $50,000. As soon as someone posted the money, I'd be free to leave. I should've said I was broke. The detectives probably would've let me go anyway since they wanted Harris, as if he were the worst drug dealer on earth.

I called my parents, but my father refused to bail me out. Instinctively, he knew I needed to sit in jail while everything cooled down. I spoke to my mom, and she eventually convinced my dad to help me. After spending a few days behind bars, I returned home with a daunting burden. I'd have to sacrifice someone else to save myself. I barely thought about the repercussions my agreement might have on my loved ones. Now I had endless questions. What if someone realized what happened? Would the police protect my family after I left? Would Tanya consider a life in hiding? If she did, would the police allow her and Carlton to join me? Could the police rearrest me? All I had to go on was their word. If something went wrong, would anyone believe me over seasoned detectives? In my haste, I selfishly thought only of my wants. I was arrested on July 30, 1992. In the following weeks, however, I'd face a fate much worse than jail.

CHAPTER SIXTEEN

HANGING ON

While in jail, I vowed to leave drugs alone. I needed the money, but I didn't want to sell for fear of what might happen. Nevertheless, I had to stay in the game to stay out of jail. I picked up where I had left off but tried to keep a low profile. I rationalized my actions by saying that I needed to act as if nothing had changed in order to gain Michael's trust. Confusion gripped me. I had moments when I wanted to shoot myself and end the turmoil. Fleeing to Seattle crossed my mind, but if I left, my parents would lose their bond money and their home.

Approximately ten days after my arrest, Tanya came back. This time she brought little Carl with her. Having Tanya and Carl nearby helped me to relax. Tanya wanted to spend time with her cousin Victoria, who lived in Decatur. When we arrived at Victoria's three-bedroom apartment, we were shocked. Her cousin shared the place with a boyfriend, four kids, and a gang of roaches. I asked if she wanted to reconsider staying there. After all, the roaches had set up shop in the tub, and the refrigerator was bare.

Although Tanya viewed cleanliness as a virtue, she decided to stay. We went to the store and returned with bleach and enough groceries to fill the refrigerator. Still, Victoria made me uncomfortable. "You got a good man," she told Tanya. "He takes care of the children and cleans up." She reminded me of the wolf who tried to eat the three little pigs. Victoria stared at me intently and sat with her legs spread open. I tried spending the night there a couple of times, but I couldn't get any rest because I couldn't tolerate the environment. The kids ran around well past midnight. They cooked around the clock, as if they were afraid the food might have disappeared.

Once we sat outside playing cards with Victoria and her boyfriend. After the game, Tanya hugged me and felt a bulge in my shirt pocket. She reached in and grabbed a bag of cocaine. "What's this?" she asked. I told her it was sugar and to give it back. She dismissed her findings, but I think by then she knew the powder's true identity. If she had any doubt, it would be erased in a few days.

August 15, 1992, began like any other day. Earlier, I hung out with Tanya at her cousin's apartment. We made love, and I told her I'd return later in the evening to take her out. When I got home, my mom said Burt stopped by. He wanted me to come get him. Since I already had plans, I brushed him off. Besides, Burt specialized in freeloading. I took a steamy shower. While I dressed, my pager beeped relentlessly. Lionel's number flashed on the screen. I called him, and he asked me to bring an ounce of crack.

"That's more cash to party with," I thought. I called my friend Hook and asked if he wanted to party tonight. He said "yes." I then called Tanya and told her I'd be by to get her in an hour, just enough time to meet Lionel, pick up Hook, and return to Decatur. As I walked to the front door, my nephew Roderick started crying and rolled over to me in his walker. He grabbed my leg. "I'll be back," I said as I picked him up. He stopped crying. When I handed him to my mom, he started crying again. "I'll be back," I repeated.

I pulled into the parking lot at the Rockpoint Apartment complex to sell crack rocks to Lionel. I pressed play on my tape deck and listened to "The End of the Road," by Boys to Men, my new favorite song. As I bobbed my head, a figure jumped into my passenger's seat. It was Lionel. From his countenance and hunched posture, I realized this wasn't an ordinary meeting. The scene unfolded rapidly.

Lionel leaned towards me with a gun, wielding it toward my face like a surgeon preparing to make an incision. "I got to have me, G," he yelled. Next, a burning sensation ran through the side of my neck as a bullet pierced it. Lionel rummaged through my pockets, took all my money, and took all the crack.

"Man, you didn't have to shoot me," I whispered, as I lay my head back and closed my eyes. I pretended like I was dead. Lionel then closed the door and ran off.

"I'm going to kick his ass," I said to myself. When I tried to move, I felt blood streaming down to my feet. The sensation felt like I was drowning in a pool of blood. "Help! Help! I've been shot. Call the police," I yelled. The windows were up, and the music was blasting. Thankfully, a woman walking her dog heard my cries. Losing blood may have distorted my perception, but it seemed like the police took an extremely long time to arrive. When they did come, they came with questions. They wanted to know what had happened. I told them I had been shot. They wanted to know by whom. I said I didn't know. Meanwhile, the police made no effort to treat my gunshot wound.

After grilling me, the police radioed for an ambulance. The paramedics asked more questions. They wanted to know my name and age. "Just get me to the hospital," I pleaded. That night seemed like a replay of my hit-and-run accident. The paramedics placed a brace on my neck, put me on the stretcher, and raced me to the emergency room. When I got there, a detective approached me. By this time, I was crying for my mother and thinking death might be a possibility.

"Shut up. You ain't gonna die," the detective yelled. "You shouldn't have been out there selling that dope." I grew silent and tried to manage the pain. The paramedics came back, put me in another ambulance, and took me to Shepherd Spinal Center. I blacked out during the ride.

I jolted awake the next morning due to a sharp pain in my penis. My sudden awakening frightened the nurse standing over my bed. "What are you doing?" I asked.

"You felt that?" she said. I told her "yes," and she explained that she was using a condom catheter to help me urinate. The plastic tube inserted in my penis would guide my urine into a plastic bag.

"I'll get up and go to the bathroom," I told her, but I couldn't move. Instantly, I knew my life would never be the same. I lay in the hospital room staring at the ceiling. Nurses came in and out of my room. Each touch of their hands hurt. Soreness permeated through every pore of my body, particularly my right arm. I screamed when they tried to lift it.

Carla was my first visitor. Back then, she rarely drove anywhere outside of Conyers or even took the expressway. So, her visit to the hospital in Atlanta meant a lot to me. "Hey, James Brown," she said in an effort to be cheerful.

My mother came next. She looked worried and disappointed, like it did following my first arrest. She verbalized her anger, saying, "You shouldn't have been out there doing what you was doing." She offered no words of encouragement or sympathy. My father and uncles followed, though M.C. didn't come. Seeing me right then would've made him break down. His son Kevin had recently been charged with drug possession and was awaiting sentencing. For him, my shooting may have felt like another blow. No one, in fact, cried or broke down during their visits. People did express their condolences in other ways. I recall receiving balloons that bore a variety of get well messages.

In between visitors, I lay in my bed thinking not of recuperation but of how I could explain what happened to Tanya. How would she react when all my secrets unfolded? The next day, I asked Carla to call Tanya and tell her about the shooting.

Tanya and Carl came. She looked to see my wound. We talked a bit though my voice was almost a whisper. I told her my father hadn't died and why I lied. "I never thought you'd accept my family and the way we live," I said. I skipped over all the other deceptions.

I lay in the intensive care unit, waiting for the doctor to see me. He entered my room with my X-rays and devastating news. "Mr. Brown, you have a .22 bullet logged in your spinal cord," he explained. "Your brain messages can't get through the bullet to tell your arms and legs to move. I'm sorry to tell you this, but you'll be paralyzed from your neck down without movement or feeling for the rest of your life." He said that if he attempted to remove the bullet, it might cause potentially fatal damage. He further explained that my large neck and physique were blessings. They slowed the bullet down, he said. Someone smaller than me probably would've died.

I looked at him and whispered, "You're a liar. I'm gonna walk again. I'm gonna walk again."

The doctor said he wished me luck and then left the room. I remember feeling so defeated and hurt. I grew weaker, and my voice faded. I used my eyes to communicate, blinking once for "yes" and twice for "no."

I remember being alone and crying a lot. Tanya stayed overnight once, but only out of a sense of obligation. I felt alone and hurt. Many nights I wanted Tanya to stay with me, but she wouldn't.

My aunt Lillie came with Bible in hand. She said that with faith in God the size of a mustard seed, I could move mountains, and with Jesus' stripes, I'd be healed. She professed that I would be healed and get up and walk again. "All you've got to do is have faith, James," she said. Lillian read scriptures and tried to inspire me with the Word.

Everyone, except me, focused on me walking again. I focused on making it through the night and facing another day. Learning how the nurses would have to do my bowel movements devastated me. They put on gloves slathered in Vaseline then placed a finger up my anus. They moved the finger around to stimulate the sphincter muscle, causing it to contract and initiate a bowel movement. To finish the procedure, the nurses pulled the bowel from my anus. At times, I wanted to die. In addition to pain medicine, the doctor prescribed Ditropan to keep me from urinating on myself and Tofranil to curb my depression.

Pape flew from Seattle to see me. His presence lifted my spirits, but I was more worried about his feelings once he discovered my lies. Pape and Tanya learned the truth about my Navy discharge when they suggested that Shepherd send me to the Veteran's Administration hospital. My parents told them I had no benefits, so they were applying for Medicaid. Seeing Pape's hurt expression distressed me. I apologized for deceiving his family. He told me he understood, and we prayed together. For the second time, Pape said he thought of me as a son. Pape stayed for a week, and when he left, he took Carl with him.

Tanya and my sister got along well, too well in fact. A couple of weeks after the shooting, they started clubbing together. They'd drop by the hospital to see me on their way out. I wanted Tanya to have a life, but knowing they were having so much fun only amplified my inability to do simple things.

Burt and Junebug visited twice. When I was selling drugs, they hung around me constantly. "Where were they now?" I thought.

Lionel's niece and her mother visited once. I told them he shot me. Later, I found out that Lionel was a crackhead, not a dealer. Without a doubt, I believe Teddy sent him my way. However, when the detective questioned me again, I told him an unknown assailant shot me, so he left me alone.

I had good and bad days. No sum of drug money could help me find my way. I called on the Lord because only He could help me out of this situation. In Him I sought the strength I lacked, the strength no relative, friend, or even Tanya could provide. I stayed in intensive care for about a week. Ten days after the shooting, I left the bed for the first time. The nurses told me I had to get up and that I couldn't lie around anymore. The nurses were firm, yet gentle. As they lifted me out of the bed, the room swirled around me. They laid me on a mat and began range of motion exercises with my legs and arms. Because my arms still felt very sore, I screamed when the nurses tried to stretch them. The physical therapy kept my joints from locking up and aided in circulation.

Tanya went back to Seattle to get her affairs in order. She did call the hospital to check on me, but we never discussed our future. With Tanya gone, I concentrated on therapy more intensely. I graduated from my bed to a sip-and-puff wheelchair. To control the chair, I sucked out of and blew into a straw attached to it. I blew one time to go forward, sucked in once to go backwards, blew twice to turn right, and sucked in twice to turn left. At first, I ran into walls and people, especially as I practiced using the elevator.

Finally the day came when the irritating neck brace came off. Since I had no use of my arms, my mouth became a substitute. The nurses placed a pen in my mouth and taught me how to write my name. For many other tasks, I learned to use a mouth stick, which looks like a small, two-prong, blunt-tipped pitch fork. Prior to being paralyzed, I wasn't computer literate. Thanks to a high school typing class, I learned how to use a keyboard.

Using the mouth stick, I typed on the computer, dialed phone numbers, and controlled television remotes.

I welcomed them, but the therapy sessions drained me. Exhausted, I always rested well after my sessions. If I missed therapy, I would only sleep four to five hours, if that. I dreaded the darkness, afraid Lionel might creep through the door and finish me off. When he robbed me, he left all my jewelry. Now the gold symbols of my excessive, criminal lifestyle were useless on my aching, swollen body. I prayed and sat thinking of how each choice I made led me to this hospital room. I rewound my life over and over and hypothesized about where different choices may have led.

CHAPTER SEVENTEEN

UNRAVELING

My six-week stay at Shepherd Spinal Center passed quickly, for I had grown fond of the caring staff. Now, I'd have to prepare for life on the outside as a C-4 quadriplegic. Towards the end of my stay, my parents faced an important decision. Because my Medicaid would end soon and I had no medical insurance, my parents would have to place me in a nursing home or care for me at home. Both choices would burden my family in some respect. Living in a nursing home would mean a lifelong financial strain on my parents. On the other hand, living back home, while less expensive, meant they would bear the responsibility of my medical needs. My mother usually served more as an advocate for my needs. Under these circumstances, however, my father made the final decision. He went against her wishes and elected to care for me at home.

We all went through a week of adjustments. I went from my room in the house to a bedroom in our garage. I blew into a tube to call for assistance in the hospital. At home, I had to yell for my parents to come help. Getting me in and out of bed was a job for two people. My mom, with the assistance of Carla or a neighbor, placed a Hoyer net on my bed and rolled me back and forth until my body fit onto the net. She then placed a Hoyer lift under the bed, connected its chains to rings on the net, hoisted me up, and dropped me into my manual wheelchair.

Medicaid only covered a basic, non-electric wheelchair. If I showed signs of improvement, they'd upgrade to a better model, but not a $30,000 sip-n-puff that I had use of at the hospital. Until then, someone would have to manually lean my wheelchair back on two wheels about every 30 minutes to keep my circulation going.

My mom never liked blood or any bodily fluids, but she became my main caregiver. She balanced her full-time job with helping me. Carla worked from 3 p.m. to 11 p.m. and slept late, but she helped me from around noon until she had to prepare for work. She did everything she could for me, but she never learned to do a catheter until years later. Instead, five times a day, my parents did my catheter. My mother bathed me each day, and she emptied my bowels every two to three days.

Nights in the garage were difficult. A cold draft sifted through the window and other crevices. I heard mice scampering around as they gnawed a hole through the plywood frame that encased the garage. Imagining that they'd crawl on me and scratch me with their tiny paws, I slept uneasily.

Within two weeks after I arrived home, my father came in the garage with a grin on his face. "I got a surprise for you, boy," he said. In walked Tanya. Although we spoke on the phone, I missed her and welcomed the company. So far, only a few friends had stopped by to visit. Burt and Junebug couldn't leave fast enough when my mom started to give me a catheter. They did visit more once they found out Tanya was in town.

Overjoyed is the only way I can describe having Tanya and Carl back. Carl climbed into bed with me during the day and slept at my side. Tanya slept with me also, and we even had sex in my wheelchair. This was not the first time since the shooting, though. We had sex in the hospital right before she left for Seattle. Soon after she returned to Atlanta this time, however, she asked for her own bed. My father brought my old bed into the garage. Eventually, she stopped being affectionate all together and even made Carl sleep with her.

Tanya and Carla resumed their club hopping even though my mother disapproved. Carla left Roderick with my mother while Tanya left Carl with me. "What are you doing taking my girl out?" I asked Carla.

Since I couldn't use my arms or legs, my mother actually bore the responsibility of both children. Tanya showed me souvenirs from her nights out: photos of other men hugging her. She claimed they were just friends. Seeing those photos hurt like hell. How could she hold a friend and not a fiancé? I knew Tanya partly came back for me, but I suspected that exploring Atlanta motivated her just as much.

To add insult to injury, Tanya declined to help my mother with my bowel movements and bathe me. Sometimes, though, Tanya did my catheter. Despite our differences, she brought me closer to Christ. "You need to read your Bible and be in the Word," Tanya said. Meanwhile, I had to yell for my parents to help me while she sat right next to me. My wheelchair had a lap table connected to where I placed my food and drinks. When I asked Tanya to hand me something to eat, she'd say, "Get your own food." When I asked for a glass of water, she'd say, "Get your water yourself."

Tanya and Carla stopped hanging out after Carl accidentally knocked Roderick down while they played outside. Roderick's head hit the concrete in front of our house, and blooded oozed so heavily from the gash that Carla had to rush him to the hospital. My parents adored Roderick, so the accident only amplified the tension in our house. Secretly, I envied the way my father treated my nephew. My father rode Roderick around in his car, took him to buy candy, and played with him in the yard. My father had every opportunity to do these same things with me, yet he chose otherwise. In a way, I think my bond with Pape made my father just as jealous.

Tanya's father visited about a month after she had arrived. He wanted to stay in my old room, but my parents wouldn't let him. I told Pape I was sorry that my parents were so inhospitable. Their refusal demonstrated one more reason why I lied about my father's death and dreaded for our families to meet. Pape told me not to worry. He attempted to spend the week at Victoria's apartment, but the roaches chased him away. Pape booked a hotel room instead. Tanya felt slighted. "I hope they don't think they got anymore than we got 'cause I'll take them to my house," she said.

In spite of my embarrassment, I valued the time Pape spent with me. He rented a minivan, invited some of my friends over and took us to the movies. Sitting in the front seat of a car never felt so good, especially after I had been restricted to my house since leaving Shepherd. Pape and

I sat in the garage talking, reading the Bible, and generally enjoying each other. Pape's parting words to me were: "Son, you can do all things through Christ, who strengthens you. The Master will never put more on you than you can bear." His presence helped me ignore the strain between the other adults in the house. When he left, though, it was business as usual.

I argued with Tanya about her behavior. Men called her and came to the house. "You know I don't get along with females," Tanya said. "Now you don't want me to have no friends?"

I was paralyzed, not stupid. I had a feeling we were doomed, still I clung to hope. My mother also saw the signs. She and Tanya bickered more and more. "She better not say nothing to me," Tanya threatened. She didn't want to eat my mom's food or use anything in the house. They always seemed to be on the verge of a blowout.

Without Carla to hang out with, Tanya spent more time with Victoria. Once I overheard them on the phone talking about me, and her cousin said, "You need to push that crippled motherfucker out the wheelchair. I don't know why you're with him. He wouldn't be hollering at me."

Tanya's mother turned against me too. I heard her urge Tanya to leave. "You need to come home because you're too young to spend your life pushing behind a wheelchair," she said.

During one of our arguments, Tanya repeated her mother's sentiments and said, "You ain't gonna find no young girl to be with you." Her words told me what I already knew. Tanya needed to save face. By coming to Conyers and staying with me, she could say she gave our relationship a valiant effort.

Tanya left just as I thought she would. The medical transport van took me to a doctor's appointment one day, and when I returned home, she was gone. No trace of her remained, not even a "Dear John Letter." She had the nerve to take some of my belongings too. Though it was inevitable, I cried and mourned her leaving. Christmas was fast approaching, and I wouldn't be able to see Carl open his gifts. I doubted Tanya would let me see him again. All my family members echoed the same sentiments. "If she wanted to be with you," they said, "she'd be here. Tanya didn't care for you. Remember when she used to go to the clubs and wouldn't even help with your bowel movements?"

My appetite decreased, and I had the biggest pity party this side of the Mississippi. My father suggested an unusual remedy for my gloominess. He invited company, of the female persuasion, to the house. I assumed they were prostitutes or crackheads. My father said the women would do anything I wanted. The last thing I needed or wanted was for my father to bring random women to me. Having sex with them wouldn't eliminate my issues. I took my anger out on my mom because she was the closest target. Besides, her treating me like a child and throwing my past in my face infuriated me. My mom told me that if I had not been selling drugs, she would not have had to take care of me. We cursed each other out. I know that stress caused us to spew hurtful words at times.

Though Lionel shot me, I blamed myself for my predicament. I had nothing but time to sit and think. I had begun reading about Job's trials, and I started remembering my early childhood and the rape. Confronting my cousin crossed my mind. I called a relative to ask if she knew his whereabouts. She told me he was in prison for molesting and raping his own children. My silence had allowed him to strike again. I told Carla and my mom what had happened. They both said they were sorry. I wanted to commit suicide, but I couldn't pull a trigger or even hold a bottle of pills. I called 10 different crackheads and offered each one $200 for my assassination. They all declined. I wanted to offer them more, but the money I had hidden in my car trunk mysteriously disappeared, so I couldn't afford a higher payment. Roscoe, my dad's friend, told my father what I had done. My father asked if I were crazy and told me to stop calling people to kill me because nobody would do it.

Without death as an alternative, I had to learn to face life on its new terms. Slowly, things started improving in my life even though I had no quick fix for my pain. Tanya was gone, but two other women would ultimately help me to get over her.

Phyllis spent two hours a day with me. She became my first nurse after Medicaid finally allotted for one. She bathed and dressed me. Having Phyllis around took some of the pressure off my mom, who was and still is my angel. Phyllis and I have kept in touch over the years. Back then, Phyllis lifted me with her voice. She sang me the gospel song "I Feel Like Going On." I wanted to jump out of the bed and give praise. Meanwhile, Aunt Lillian continued using God's Words to heal my broken spirit. She even brought some of her church folks to visit me sometimes. The garage became a makeshift worship center. We'd sing, pray, and give glory to God. Their visits broke my daytime talk show routine and gave me something to look forward to.

My dad bought a van to take me to my appointments. He created a ramp with a large piece of wood and rolled me into the van. Roscoe often rode with us. Dr. Lee examined me and said I needed to be in physical therapy. My fingers had curled up due to inactivity. Before I left the hospital, he had given my parents instructions for range of motion exercises, but they focused only on my basic needs. Dr. Lee also noticed my weight loss and look of despair. I told him how miserable I was. He said my experiences were normal and many patients find out who their friends are during trying times. I rejected seeing a psychologist, so Dr. Lee prescribed more Tofranil and suggested that I get out of the house more. I wasn't crazy, but I felt like I might have been on the verge of a breakdown.

I agreed with Dr. Lee that I needed a change of scenery and pace. Consequently, I began eagerly attending therapy sessions at Shepherd. While there, I used an automated weight machine that exercised my arms and legs. The Shepherd staff encouraged me to get out and do things in addition to therapy. I wanted to go places, but my manual chair limited my mobility because I had to rely on someone to push me around. Moreover, every two hours, someone had to adjust and recline me so I wouldn't get sores on my butt. Weeks after therapy started, I got slight movement back in my left hand. It was enough to move a wheelchair joystick. The doctor applied to Medicaid for a motorized chair. Shortly before Christmas, I received an early present: a new wheelchair.

Finally, I could move about and recline myself. The new chair signified freedom. I rolled outside and practiced maneuvering the chair. I rode on the driveway and sometimes got off course, venturing into the gravel. Riding on the gravel was difficult and rough at first. After practicing a bit, I felt confident. I got stuck, but I never fell.

Unraveling

The more I moved closer to God, the more I battled with devilish thoughts. Self-pity became my new vice, and I shifted from seeing the chair as a gift to seeing it as a way to end my misery. I hated the burden I imposed on my family. My mother left Sears because it was relocating. She could've worked at the new location, but she quit instead. If she didn't have me to worry about, I felt, she probably would've kept working. I grappled with the mess I had made of my life and those close to me. I looked down at my disfigured hands. The hands that once gripped a football could now only control a wheelchair joystick.

I decided to use my limited dexterity to end it all. Cars flew up and down the street constantly. Because of a blind spot, they wouldn't see me coming in my chair. With one push, all my pain could end. I just had to time the collision precisely. As I prepared my demise one day and began to roll into the street, I heard a voice say, "Try me."

I stopped and listened.

CHAPTER EIGHTEEN

SEEKING FORGIVENESS AND FINDING FAITH

Instantly, I knew I had heard God's voice. He answered my call, but in my mind, a little too late. Foolishly, I questioned Him. "Where were you when I was being raped? Where were you when my daddy would beat my momma? Where were you on August 15, 1992, the night I got shot? Where were you when I needed you the most?"

God spoke back, "Where were you when I made the heavens and earth? Where were you when I took dirt from the ground to make Adam and took a rib from him to make Eve?" he answered. "I was with you the whole time. I carried you for a specific purpose in life, and I'm going to use you in a special way."

I had no idea how God's plan would unfold, but I trusted His word. I rolled back in the house, prayed, and read the Bible. Somewhere between Genesis and Revelations, I searched for a cure for my paralysis. During prayer, I found the next best thing: forgiveness. I thanked God and sought his forgiveness for selling drugs, disrespecting my mother, and committing the other wrongs. As I sought forgiveness, I gave it. I forgave my cousin for raping me. I forgave Lionel for shooting me, and I forgave Tanya for leaving me.

God continued to speak to me. We had many late night conversations. He picked up the broken pieces of my life and brought me the joy and peace that the drug game had snatched away. God said, "You don't feel as if you've had the best relationship with your father, so call me father. "Your friends have deserted you. I'll be your running partner. Tanya left you, but I'll send someone to love you for whom you are."

With my burdens lifted, I transformed my thoughts from the limitations of paralysis to my abilities. "I can go on and live life victoriously in this chair," I said to myself. "I'm gonna focus on James." So, I began to venture out. My father dropped me off at J.P. Carr so I could watch the basketball games. I saw Junebug, but he looked right past me without saying word. I saw other friends in the street, and they, too, acted as if they didn't know me. Dwight came over sometimes and bathed me or gave me a catheter. Occasionally, my father let Dwight borrow the van, and he'd take me places. In a way, he became a substitute big brother. Thomas wanted to come back to Conyers and find Lionel after the shooting, but uncle A.W. dissuaded him. Seeking revenge would only lead to more heartache.

I asked my father to drop me off on Sundays at Antioch Baptist Church, where my Aunt Lillian's worshipped. Antioch provided a refreshing atmosphere, and the congregation showed me love. Unlike my home church, Antioch was wheelchair accessible. One Sunday we had dinner in the reception hall. I wheeled myself into the room and eyed plates piled high with chicken, macaroni and cheese, and collard greens. I wanted to eat but couldn't feed myself, so I milled around meeting new people. A young lady named Dashawn walked over to me and struck up a conversation. I asked her to feed me, and she did. Dashawn introduced me to her friend Teresa. I also met Teresa's family that day. Dashawn asked if they could come visit me. Since my social calendar lacked events, I told her yes. Dashawn said she would cook for me and asked what I liked. I told her I loved dressing.

Less than a week later, I sat in the garage watching television when I unexpectedly felt a presence by my side. I turned to find Teresa leaning in to kiss my cheek. She startled me. My sudden movement caused our lips to connect. Rather than a peck, we had a full kiss. I looked at Teresa, and she looked at me. Just then, Dashawn walked in the room. They had called my mother to arrange the surprise. We sat in the garage talking. I appreciated that they looked beyond my wheelchair. I learned a little about them both. Teresa was 18, had a daughter, and didn't work although she graduated high school. She fit the profile of my previous girlfriends. Teresa lived with her parents, and our fathers had been schoolmates. I began concentrating mostly on Teresa. Dashawn faded into the background.

Teresa gave me her phone number. I called her to arrange another visit. Since she couldn't drive, Carla picked her up. When they pulled up to the house, paramedics were loading me into an ambulance. They followed me to the hospital. Teresa and her daughter, Diana, sat in the hospital room with me while the doctor gave me medicine to treat a urinary tract infection. We returned to my house afterward.

From that point on, Teresa visited me several times a week. Her visits led to dating. Teresa said she liked our conversations, but we also had an intense physical attraction. My wheelchair didn't intimidate her. Even a quick glance could lead to a sexual interlude. Tanya's prediction that a young woman would never want me was wrong. Less than a year after Tanya deserted me, Teresa's actions proved her wrong. Teresa wanted me as a friend and a lover.

I continued my physical therapy and gained more arm strength. The small improvement led me to believe I could regain substantial usage of at least one arm. Armed with that hope, I sought other avenues for physical restoration. Through the Shepherd grapevine, I heard of a recovery program in Warm Springs. People said the water there healed President Theodore Roosevelt's polio and freed him from his wheelchair. Certainly, I could benefit from those healing waters. I told Teresa about my discovery. For eight weeks, if approved, I would attend the Independent Living Program. The program's sponsors would cover all my basic needs: housing, food and nurses. Teresa encouraged me to apply. On the other hand, my mother thought I shouldn't. Despite my disability, I wanted the confidence to go out and do things for myself. I had to find ways to live independent of my parents. I didn't want to spend my life in the garage.

I gained admittance to the program shortly after signing up. My dad and Roscoe drove me to Warm Springs, a two-hour drive from Conyers. At this point, my father and I were getting along better. I knew he carried guilt because he introduced me to the drug dealing scene. Initially, some of my relatives blamed him for my shooting. He mentioned their accusation after I returned home from the hospital, but I told him I faulted myself. He presented the opportunity to take responsibility, but I made the choice to accept it instead. On the way to Warm Springs, I suggested to my dad that he stop dealing, but he brushed off my concerns. For the remainder of the ride, I listened to my dad's favorite songs and gazed at the scenery. Compared to Conyers, the trees surrounding Warm Springs looked almost majestic. I breathed in the fresh scent of pine. In fact, the closer we drew to the facility, the fresher the air seemed. In the distance, I spotted mist rising from the springs. As we inched towards the entrance, a colorful burst of flowers greeted us.

Warm Spring's appeared to be a perfect place for renewal. The natural setting reminded me that all of nature — flowers, trees, and humans alike — goes through seasons of change. I anticipated my change, learning to live independently despite my wheelchair. In the lobby, countless wheelchair-bound people rolled around. At Shepherd, most of the patients I had seen were recuperating, but the people I saw now looked vibrant. I signed in and proceeded to my room. Freddie, my roommate, had gotten there the day before. He reminded me of myself at my lowest point. I think God arranged our room assignment. His wife left him, and he wasn't receiving help at home. I tried to uplift Freddie, telling him I wasn't fully recovered but was a lot better than I used to be. Once he let the thought of losing his wife go, I told him, he'd feel better. I told Freddie the hurt wouldn't instantly disappear, but he'd start to feel relieved.

Freddie's predicament made me value my family even more. We had our differences, but they made sure I was clean and fed each day. Besides Freddie and me, there were approximately eight other program participants. Freddie, unfortunately, remained stagnant during our stay. He couldn't get over his wife's betrayal. I, on the other hand, thrived. The facility, a three-story building that was set up like a small hospital, was totally wheelchair accessible. I took pleasure in being able to use tables, doors, and bathrooms that were fitted to my needs. I had a nurse's station on my floor where I could call if I needed help. However, I basically operated on a schedule, telling the staff when I wanted to eat and bathe. I hadn't been in a shower since I left Shepherd. Now, I took one almost every day. The nurse placed me on a stretcher and showered me. Feeling water bounce off my skin felt really refreshing. Something as simple as a shower made me think of the little things I had taken for granted.

The Independent Living program revolved around a series of therapy sessions, classroom studies, and real-world exercises. I particularly enjoyed water therapy. There was a large heated pool filled with spring water where we did range of motion exercises. With all these exercises, normal feeling returned to my entire body except for my left arm, which I used to control my chair. Before I went to the program, I felt painful sensations in some body parts and nothing in others. My nephew used to bite me and put ice on my arm in an effort to test if I felt anything.

In the classroom, our teachers taught us practical lessons on how to live independently with disabilities. They stressed the power of saying "please" and "thank you." I had always known to say these words, but I would forget to use them on occasion. The teachers motivated the patients to go out into their communities. We learned what to avoid on sidewalks and in buildings, as well as to become more in tune with all our surroundings. The teachers also suggested that we should be advocates for people living with disabilities. Whenever possible, they said we should offer suggestions to community leaders and business owners to help improve accessibility for disabled citizens. They encouraged us to be confident and to meet new people.

To practice our independent living strategies, we went to Atlanta and rode the Marta trains. We stopped at various places and learned how to move about in our chairs. The teachers even showed us how to eat in public and showed us the best places to sit in restaurants. One day I rolled to a nearby restaurant. I asked a lady in line if she'd feed me in exchange for a free meal. She agreed. Later in class, I bragged of my success. Throughout the eight-week program, I became more relaxed and self-assured.

Next to the building where I stayed, was a school for people who had mental challenges and behavioral problems. Everyone shared the cafeteria, however. I met Reggie, who attended the school, while I was rolling around the grounds. I made the mistake of calling him a "dwarf." He quickly corrected my blunder, "I'm a little person," he uttered. Reggie noticed I needed a haircut and offered to give me one for $5. He put his little chair against mine, jumped on it, and clipped away. We became buddies. Reggie was funny and mischievous.

I also met Tony, whose wife had allegedly placed a contract on his life so she could collect his insurance money. The men she apparently hired followed Tony, dragged him from his truck, beat him with baseball bats, poured gasoline on him, and set him on fire. "Hell, I guess she said I was worth more dead than alive," Tony joked. As he spoke, I imagined having to smell my flesh burn. Just the nubs of Tony's fingers remained. His face looked like a melted candle, and both his legs had been amputated. Compared to some of the people I met, my suffering was minimal.

Throughout my stay, I called Teresa. She acted distant and different than her talkative self. "I've done this before," I thought. A medical transport van picked me up from Warm Springs and took me to Teresa's. I asked her what was wrong. Finally, she confessed to sleeping with Destiny's father and becoming pregnant again. They later married. To avoid Teresa and her husband, I stopped going to Antioch. Though the courtship hadn't reached the level of my involvement with Tanya, I missed Teresa. I often wondered how and what she was doing. My time at Warm Springs helped me overcome my disappointment, though. It taught me that trials can slow me down, but they don't have to stop me.

CHAPTER NINETEEN

STARTING OVER

With renewed determination, I focused on gaining my life back and living independently. I wanted to improve my communication skills and set out beyond my comfort zone. I had my father drop me off at the Marta station. I went to the Underground and started meeting people. I'd have my mom do my catheter before I left. Sometimes, I'd go out without eating, determined to find someone to feed me. I wore a brace on my arm that had a splint made into it. I'd carry a credit card or money in the splint. I also had a large backpack on the rear of my chair where I kept my wallet for any purchases I made. When I shopped, I had the cashier take out the wallet, count the money in front of me, and put the wallet back. I didn't focus on the possibility that someone might try to rob me. My bag was securely attached to the chair. Between my loud voice and my improved steering capabilities, I thought I could make a speedy escape or at least scare off a thief. The power of "please" and "thank you" usually worked, although every now and then, I approached someone who sneered at me as if I were subhuman.

In 1994, I got an unexpected and unwelcome phone call. Lionel turned himself in because the police had been relentlessly going to his mother's house. Thanks to a jailhouse snitch, he emerged as their main suspect in my shooting. Still, Lionel declared his innocence. I had hoped to never hear about or face Lionel again.

Throughout my life, I learned to block out painful episodes. The shooting was no exception. Memories of that night constantly flooded back. I questioned why Lionel turned himself in. How could he claim to be innocent? Two weeks before he surrendered, my father had taken me to a rundown Atlanta apartment complex. We entered one unit to find a grey-haired woman with weathered skin. On the table in front of her sat a Bible. I suspected she supplied the necklace my father wore for protection. She asked me what happened to me. Without giving a detailed account, I told her I got shot. "Don't you worry about him, honey," she said. "He's a dirty nigga. We gonna get him." She also told me I'd walk again. I didn't want to think about Lionel, but I did hope her other prediction was correct.

The detective who questioned me at the hospital requested that I come to a deposition. During the meeting, I admitted Lionel shot me. Teddy's girlfriend and a guy I had met while selling to Lionel were also present. Being in the room with them made me uncomfortable, to say the least. The trial would be in June, almost six months later. Charged with attempted murder, Lionel faced 20 years in prison. After the deposition, I received threatening phone calls. The caller would breathe into the phone, hang up, or say "kill, kill, kill." Knowing that I had to face Lionel messed with my mind. I couldn't think clearly. The pending trial caused me to become anxious and to lose focus. I slept less at night. Attorneys, whom I thought, at the time, represented the state, came to my house to question me. I didn't expect their visit, but my father let them in to the garage. They asked questions regarding my background and the shooting. I told them about everything, including my drug charge. Somehow, I thought forgetting about Lionel would cause him to forget about me. Now, the police had opened a chapter I tried to close.

The trial finally began. It lasted less than a week. Lionel's family glared at me as I rolled into the courtroom. I had no friends or relatives in court. Suspicious thoughts raced through my mind. Anything could happen in the courtroom. Junebug, who was in jail, told my brother's old friend Dwayne that he had seen Lionel reading law books. "Would the police try to turn this on me?" I pondered. I mistrusted the detective because of how he treated me directly after the shooting. When Lionel shot me, I saw the devil. In the courtroom, I saw him again. My apprehension increased when I realized Lionel's lawyers were the men who visited my house. When they questioned me, I said, "You all said you were from the district attorney's office." I already knew what Lionel was capable of and didn't want him to retaliate. I admitted that he shot me but lied about everything else. His attorney's were using my own words against me. They did an excellent job of creating reasonable doubt. His attorney's insinuated that someone I had sold to before or someone present at the card game when I got arrested may have shot me. Again, I pretended to be a user, not a dealer. When the prosecutor asked me to show him who shot me, I rolled over and faced the devil. "It was him," I said, pointing at Lionel.

A couple of days later, the verdict came in: not guilty. My nervousness increased and so did the calls. I relied on prayer to help me cope. Gradually, the calls stopped. An old classmate of mine was a jury member. I ran into him one day. He told me that he had failed to disclose that he knew me. Due to inconsistencies in my story, he said, the jury found Lionel innocent. Seven months later, Lionel reaped what he sowed. He robbed a video store and assaulted the clerk. He received a 40-year prison sentence. Eventually, I dusted myself off and moved on. I resumed my quest for independent living. While watching television, a commercial for Advanced Career Travel School caught my attention. The school trained its students to become travel agents. "I do miss traveling," I thought. I decided that opening a travel agency could be a career and a way for me to travel inexpensively. I was certain I could perform the job, for I typed and answered phones as well as anyone else.

I called the state's vocational rehabilitative services office. The office helps the disabled reenter the workforce. A counselor came to interview me and discuss my goals. I told him I wanted to own a business. He said I needed realistic goals. "Because I'm in a chair, you don't think I can open my own business?" I asked. He didn't budge, so I said I wanted to be a travel agent instead. What I didn't say is that I still planned on opening an agency. He tested my math and reading skills and then agreed to pay for the training.

My counselor sent a van to take me to ACT. I went to the front desk and asked the receptionist for an application. "Who do you want to get it for?" she asked. I told her it was for me. She stared at me up and down as if to say, "What are you doing here?"

The receptionist placed the application on the desk. "Sir," she said, "how are you going to write, do everything you need to do, and type at least 30 wpm on the low end?"

I stared back and said, "I've got a stick. I type with my mouth stick just as fast as people who use their hands." She paged the school's director to come to the front desk. The director made me show them what I could do. She took my mouth stick from the splint and gave it to me. I typed on a lap keyboard. They both told me they had never seen any one use a mouth stick before. My swift and accurate typing shocked them. The school had never had a wheelchair-bound applicant. Impressed, they filled out the application for me.

I hired Yvonne, a lady my father knew, to attend class with me and take notes. For nine months, we went to classes five days a week. During the same time, I wanted to give my mom her life back. School had been the first step. I loved my parents but needed to feel like an adult and run my own household. My income was so small that I couldn't afford an apartment, though. Disabled people in my situation had to live in nursing homes, with relatives, or with friends. While I considered my living options, I heard about a paralyzed woman who was protesting in front of the governor's office. Like me, she didn't want to live in a nursing home. Therefore, I joined the protest, rolling around with picket signs attached to my wheelchair. If passed, the waiver would allow disabled Georgians to apply for subsidized nursing care in their homes.

I couldn't wait on the waiver, so I looked for a place to stay. My options were limited, though. As a result, I took the first place I could afford, a two-story townhouse not far from my parents. I planned to get a roommate to live upstairs to help with the rent. My father loaded up the van. I only had a few belongings, which made the move easy. The first night I moved in, I immediately grasped the enormity of my decision. I couldn't yell for my parents if I needed anything, and a nurse would stop by only for a short time. My parents came by to check on me, but I still felt lonely. I started talking on a chat line and met Kelly, a 19-year-old girl. We became friends. She even attended school with me a couple of times. Kelly wanted to go to nursing school, so I taught her how to take care of me. I suggested that she become my roommate. Kelly agreed to come if she could bring her niece, who was a little younger than she. I agreed.

On the day Kelly moved in, she knocked on the door and said she had a surprise. She went outside and came back with a baby. Kelly claimed she had adopted him from her cousin. "How can a 19-year-old adopt a baby?" I asked her. She swore she had legally adopted him and said he'd be so quiet that I'd forget he was there. I loved my nephew, but the racket he made was one of the reasons I moved. "You know I don't like no noise," I told her. Kelly told me not to worry. Almost instantly, the baby started crying. Kelly said he needed some milk, so she left for the store and said she'd be right back.

Before Kelly left, she put the baby upstairs with her niece. He stopped crying. Twenty minutes later Kelly pounded on the door. Her niece, who locked the door, had fallen asleep and didn't wake up until early the next morning. I yelled throughout the night trying to wake her. Kelly slept outside. While I was screaming for Kelly's niece, the comprehension that I was paralyzed really hit me. I couldn't do anything but wait for some-one else to help. What if this had been an emergency? The next day I went to school looking like I had been boozing. Classmates even commented on my red eyes. When I returned home, no one was there, and the door was unlocked. I hadn't given Kelly a key yet. At this point, I rethought my decision to move. Later that night, they finally came back. I still thought our arrangement might work. Kelly lifted me into bed and went upstairs. Then, somebody knocked on the door. I knew it wasn't my family be-cause they usually call first. Kelly ran down the stairs and let a strange older man in the door. She introduced him, and then they went upstairs. A few minutes later, Kelly went into the kitchen. I smelled the steak and rice I had bought cooking. I also saw her pass by with my 2 liter soda. "What are you doing, girl?" I asked. "You brought some strange man over here?" She claimed the man was her uncle, but I knew better.

The next day I yelled and yelled for Kelly, but she didn't come. Luckily, it wasn't a school day. I called my mom and asked her to come do a catheter. As soon as my mom arrived, Kelly woke up. After my mom left, Kelly gave me a bath. I then left for the Marta station. While I was out, I had time to think, so I decided our arrangement wouldn't work. As soon as I returned home, I told Kelly, who said she understood. In her absence, my father came by to help when the nurse wasn't there, mainly at night.

By this time, my brother Thomas had moved back to Conyers. While he was away, he had an unsuccessful attempt in rehab. Still, I got him a job with the transportation company that took me to school. Thomas dropped me off at school one morning but never returned. I waited more than five hours for another driver to come. Thomas' boss had given him his first paycheck. He stole the van and went to a crack house where he smoked away his earnings. His addiction made him forget his own brother. Seeing Thomas on a smoking binge saddened me, but I couldn't take on his burden. At best, I could comment on his actions and support him when he decided to change.

A month after Kelly left, Dwayne came to stay with me. I trusted Dwayne and felt at ease with him there. Having a stable living arrangement helped me concentrate on my studies. In June of 1995, I graduated and finished in the top 10 percent of my class. Now I had all the training I needed to become a certified agent, but I wanted more. The school's director was so impressed that she offered to hire me, but I declined. I started researching business opportunities. Using a reference list the school provided, I called different contacts. I learned about Mrs. Russell, a travel agency owner. I told her I wanted to be self-employed. Mrs. Russell told me I could run an agency from my home. As an independent contractor for her, I earned commission for each reservation. Mrs. Russell sold me a computer program that routed calls to my phone and allowed me to book reservations. The state helped me with funds to set up a home office. Mrs. Russell printed business cards and envelopes for my agency. I named it Payback Travel Agency because I wanted to payback everyone who had helped me along the way. I also wanted to show people who said I would never amount to anything that I could be successful. I had to do my own marketing, which pretty much involved soliciting people through word of mouth and handing out business cards.

Dwayne stayed with me for almost a year before he moved out to live with his girlfriend. He occasionally came by, but our friendship ended when he refused to pay the bill for a cell phone I had loaned him. Still, God sent a new companion my way. I met her at South Dekalb Mall. Her name was Shonda, and we hit it off really well. She wanted to be a certified nursing assistant. I told her I couldn't pay much, but I could train her how to take care of me. Shonda said all she needed was $20 for gas. On weekends, she drove an hour roundtrip to bathe me and put me in my chair.

Six months later, the state waiver passed. I could have a nurse whenever I needed one. At first, I hired people I knew instead of going through an agency. Shonda worked for me full time when she wasn't in school. In fact, she ended up working for me for seven years. My sister also wanted to work for me, which was shocking. Part of me thought she'd mess up my catheter, but I gave her a chance.

With school over and my business growing, my income increased. I lived comfortably, just as any working, able-bodied person might. Reminiscent of my drug dealing days, money made me feel powerful. People, especially women, stopped viewing me as crippled. Now that I wore designer clothes instead of flea market clothes, they found me attractive and look past the wheelchair.

Rather than maximizing the blessings God had bestowed upon me, I veered further from his will. I should've been advancing and fulfilling my purpose in my life. I moved backwards instead, reconnecting with old friends and old habits.

COURAGE IN CRISES

CHAPTER TWENTY

MOVING IN REVERSE

I took my talks with God seriously. However, I failed to recognize that He speaks to us and teaches lessons by bringing certain circumstances and people into our lives. Like any good teacher, God repeats His lessons until the student learns. I had watched my brother, Thomas, battle his crack addiction without acknowledging that I had several addictions of my own: power, money and sex, or PMS.

This fact became evident when I met Mac Momma. She was a nurse who liked to party. I found pleasure in watching her cook as she danced around the kitchen shaking her butt and then dropping it low to the ground. She definitely knew how to move her body. I asked why she danced all the time. Mac Momma said she trained dancers and had a lot of girls working for her in strip clubs. The girls were runaways who stripped to stay off the street. I proposed that we become business partners. I told her I knew a lot of guys who liked to drink. Since we both liked money, we could make a profit by hooking her girls up with my guys.

My place became a hot spot. Instead of peddling crack, I now peddled girls, alcohol, and food. I had my dad travel to Griffin and buy corn liquor. The clear liquid had a deceivingly sweet taste, which caused many visitors to drink until they got drunk. I also stocked up on beer. Next, I hired one of my aunts and one of my nurses to cook. I sold collards, macaroni and cheese, ribs, chicken, and pork chops. Anybody who didn't buy a drink or food had to leave. Some people simply came for the food and left. Most of the men, expectantly, stayed to watch the entertainment. Mac Momma's girls pranced around in skimpy outfits. I rented out my upstairs bedroom for $25 per half hour. I never saw what went on up there, but I could only imagine. I had someone posted upstairs to make sure no one stayed longer than scheduled. Ironically, my house motto was: "What goes on in my house stays in my house."

Traffic in my house lined the street on Sundays, and my neighbors complained. The police came by a couple of times to tell us to quiet down. Mac Momma and I made a good $1,500 profit for each party. In the midst of all of this, Tanya called unexpectedly. She wanted to know how my family and I were doing. I told her I had just graduated and started a business. From that point, we spoke on and off for months. Tanya eventually asked if she could visit. I agreed and planned for her to come in the spring of the following year. I bought plane tickets for both Tanya and her sister Bridget. I still refer to the visit as "My ten terrible days of Tanya." This time, a new James greeted her, someone who had finally been freed from her spell.

Mistakenly, I let my nurses off because I thought Tanya would take care of me. I figured that because she was working as a patient care tech, she knew how to do everything I needed. Tanya, however, complained about me letting my nurses go. She could help strangers, but not me. My mother stopped by, and Tanya acted salty, still holding a grudge. We had sex one time, but I didn't feel connected to her anymore. She seemed too eager, as if she had an agenda. Sensing it, I almost offered to change Tanya's ticket so she could leave early. Not being able to do anything right by her standards and knowing she wanted me to take care of her made me miserable. I had a van take us to downtown Atlanta because I got tired of being cooped up with Tanya and her sister. Tanya had an attitude the entire time, and it worsened as the weekend grew near.

Tanya and her sister arrived on a Thursday. Leading up to Sunday, people kept knocking on my door. My sister came and took them to church on Sunday. When they returned, my party was in full swing. "You let all these people in and out of your house?" she asked. "You came from the Navy to this?" Tanya loved to party, and now was her chance.

Shortly before Tanya left, she mentioned that she liked Georgia and that she might bring Carl back and move in with me. Her split personality irritated me. Tanya smiled, hugged, and kissed me before she departed. When she arrived home, she called me to say she made it in safely. After Tanya's visit, I stopped accepting her calls.

For a brief moment, Tanya's criticisms forced me to look at my actions. After considering the source, I disregarded her concerns although I knew they were valid. Stopping my parties would mean letting go of the money and the attention it spawned. I needed this income to subsidize my chat line calls. I met about 50 women on the chat line and slept with about 20 of them. For many women, my chair prompted curiosity. They wanted to experience sex with a paralyzed man. I met the women at the mall, their homes, my place, or even at church. Some nights I fell asleep with two women at my side.

I was engaging in the same behavior that got me in my chair. It seemed that only a reenactment of the night Lionel shot me could slow me down again. One of the dancers, Candy, would come by my apartment just to buy corn liquor. One night she wanted to buy my entire stock. As payment, Candy plunked down a pound of marijuana on my table. "Are you trying to get somebody fed time?" I asked. "Where did you get that from?" Candy said she met a guy who liked her. When he fell asleep, she took the weed and ran. We swapped – my liquor for her weed. I had a new product. I called over some friends who knew how to cut marijuana. They put the weed in bags so I could sell it.

Word spread that I had good weed. Unfortunately, not everyone wanted to make a purchase. Some wanted to steal it. One night after Carla left my apartment, I turned off my television and sat in darkness. I was talking on the phone when I felt metal against my head. "Where the weed and money at?" I heard a young male voice say.

"It's in the closet," I whispered. I heard another person walk to the closet. The alarm went off. Carla swore she didn't set it. The buzzing frightened the boys and they ran off. The alarm company dispatched the police, who came asking questions. I told them at least two guys came through and put a gun to my head. I didn't disclose my illegal activities. The next day I disposed of all my wares.

I had already been shot because I wanted fast money, so I knew I had to leave that lifestyle alone. People still came by expecting a party, but over time the knocks stopped. I got bored easily, so I still talked on the chat line, which generated a series of short-lived relationships.

Marissa Williams, an older nurse, helped me discover a newer, more beneficial pastime. She mentioned me to her husband. He had a staff of employees who worked to employ veterans. When we met, Mr. Williams said my voice reminded him of Martin Luther King. He respected that I worked despite my disability. I hid the sordid details of my past and simply shared my more recent accomplishments. Mr. Williams arranged speaking engagements and then rented banquet halls and hotel rooms where crowds could gather to hear my story. I volunteered my services, but he wanted to make me a paid employee. Mr. Williams invited me to an awards banquet. He wanted to honor my efforts and thank me for showing veterans that fruitful life existed outside of the military and that even self-employment opportunities existed. I didn't show up for the first banquet because I felt like a fraud. Marissa had moved on by this time, so I didn't have to face her after I stood up her husband.

I finally purchased my own van. Now I could travel around without having to call the transportation company or inconvenience my dad. On weekends, my cousins and I rode to Mirage, 112 and other Atlanta nightclubs. I spun around on the dance floor and knocked the heck out of people sometimes. We'd be the first to arrive and the last to leave. I tried to enjoy living as a single man but without all the drama I had before.

One day I went to the mall and met a short, brown-skinned girl. I handed her a business card and told her to give me a call. Two months later Christina called, but I didn't remember her. When she came over, I still didn't remember her, but I'll never forget her. "I want to get to know you, kick it with you," she said. Christina worked at Blue Cross Blue Shield and lived in a suburb north of Atlanta. We were both lonely and looking to settle down. I'd visit Christina because her car had been stolen. She invited me to New Birth Baptist Church, which became my home church years later. The way the preacher analyzed the scriptures in layman's terms energized me. Christina had a caring soul, but she was high maintenance. If we went to the store for one item, she'd fill the whole shopping cart. If I took her to by one pair of shoes, she'd want two.

Christina's inability to manage money frustrated me. I suggested that she budget better, but sometimes I indulged Christina because she really adored me. I could tell by the look in her eyes. Sometimes, though, Christina's eyes had a crazed look in them. My parents liked her, and my mom said Christina was "the one." Christina wanted to be with me all the time and said she could be with me more if she had a car. I thought we were together enough already, but I wouldn't miss the long drive to her apartment. She asked me to go car shopping with her. We went to Lexus, GM, Cadillac, all over. Christina would test drive a car then say she didn't want it. At one lot, I decided to roll near the finance manager's door. I overheard their conversation. "I'm sorry," he said, "but since you had that repossession, you're going to have to come up with money down." All along, she had been lying.

I confronted Christina when she exited the office. She claimed the lie was to keep me from thinking poorly of her. We continued shopping, and she finally found a Nissan Maxima, but she needed a $5,000 down payment. Of course, she asked me for a loan. I made her promise to repay it. Every day after Christina bought the car, she came to my place. As promised, Christina started making payments. "Are we gonna take this to another level?" she asked. I said "yes" but had no idea what I was promising. Christina eventually stopped making payments, telling me I knew she couldn't afford the loan. She offered to work it off by taking care of me sexually and otherwise. I wasn't interested.

Behaviors Christina previously displayed now aggravated me, the least of which was her refusal to budget. I often heard Christina vomiting and thought that she might be sick or pregnant. Christina also brushed her hair continuously. I subsequently discovered that she was bulimic and obsessive compulsive. Christina had been overweight and feared she might become fat again. Our relationship gradually fizzled, but I harbored no ill feelings. My time with Christina taught me that we all have flaws. Choosing to ignore or overcome them is what sets each of us apart.

CHAPTER TWENTY-ONE

LIFE ENDS AND BEGINS

On December 5, 2000, my phone rang just after midnight. My sister's boyfriend said he was coming to get me. I told him I wasn't going anywhere, but that was before I noticed the Caller ID that read: Rockdale Hospital. "What's wrong?" I asked, fearing the answer.

"It's your old man," he said. "He died of a heart attack." Instantly, I remembered giving Tanya the same message about my father while I was in the Navy. The realization of this coincidence caused my heart to sink. When we reached the hospital, we asked a nurse to show us the body. She led us to the room. We entered and walked toward a body bag lying on a stretcher. My sister unzipped it slowly, revealing our father's face. It looked frozen, as if all warmth fled his body the moment he died.

Friends and family stopped by to check on me, and everyone asked if I was alright. In an effort to be strong for Carla and my mother, I exhibited none of the usual signs of grief. More than anything, I wanted to get away from the constant reminders and talk about death. So, the next night, I went to a nightclub. Surrounding myself with people who knew nothing about me provided a release.

I skipped the wake but attended the funeral. When I peered into my father's casket, I saw an older version of myself. I sat in the corner looking at the mourners and wondering where were the people my father helped during his life. My dad's friend Roscoe came and so did my half brother, Frank. Not counting immediate family and Carla's boyfriend, few people cried. Fewer even spoke. I continued masking my emotions though internally I drowned in tears. I cried for the boy who never played catch with his father and for the father who never saw his son play football. I cried because we had never hugged. I cried because I never even saw him kiss or hug my mother.

I believe my mother did the very best she knew how in raising me, but there was something missing that I so desperately needed from my father. He died before I got it from him. I had some issues that he needed to help me understand. I needed to know what it means to be a man and a husband.

My father became my best friend during the last nine months his life. We ceased arguing, and he'd sit with me in my apartment or call me on the phone. We talked a lot but never got around to saying "I love you."

My father's death led me to question my life. What would be my legacy if I had died in 1992? Would anybody have cried, come to my funeral, or cared? What would they say about me if they spoke – that I was the life of the party? What had I done with the opportunities God gave me? Thinking of my father's death and mulling over my unfulfilled life made me ill. For almost a week, I barely ate. A cloud of gloominess hung over me.

In February of the next year, I checked into Shepherd Spinal Center to have my doctor close the bedsores on my derrière. The rather routine surgery consisted of doing a skin flap, which involved removing muscle from my leg and placing it over the sore.

After surgery, I slept in a recovery room. When the nurse tried to wake me, I failed to respond. She tried so much smelling salt that she almost passed out from the scent. I had stopped breathing. The doctors rushed me to the emergency room, where they stuck a long breathing tube down my nose. I bolted awake. "We almost lost you," the doctor said. The anesthesiologist had administered too much anesthesia.

For the next five days, I laid in ICU eating nothing but chipped ice while the doctor kept me under observation. After that, I went to a regular room to continue recovery. The skin flap was unsuccessful, so I couldn't leave. My seemingly never-ending hospital stay led to more feelings of depression as I dealt with mental and physical issues. One day my blood pressure would skyrocket, the next day it would plummet. The doctors used antibiotics and ice packs to treat me although they couldn't explain my condition. I returned to ICU weak and slightly incoherent. I heard the monitor beeps decrease as my blood pressure dropped. The nurses looked at me, and I could see something was wrong in their faces.

My case manager came, followed by my mother and sister. I spoke to them, but judging from their expressions, my words made no sense. Then I blacked out. I heard God's voice more clearly now than ever before. He told me to tell my story, and God would bless me. I awoke and remained in ICU for two more days. I heard someone say, "James, the dead has risen." Everyone said I had been talking out the side of my neck, screaming, shouting hallelujah, and hollering for my mom. I'm sure my medications made me hallucinate somewhat, but I don't doubt God's presence or our conversation.

I returned to my room, waiting for the sore to heal. My roommate played one of Les Brown's motivational tapes. As I listened, I heard Les say, "You don't have to be great to get started, but you have to get started to be great." Years ago, God spoke to me through Marissa's husband, but I ignored the call. Now, I had lost contact with the Williamses. Listening to Les again inspired me to use my voice as a device for lifting the curse of drugs from my family and others. In June, the doctor released me.

A week later, one of Carla's church members requested that I speak on Youth Day. Not only did I have a large speaking engagement handed to me, but it would be in front of people whom I knew. I was nervous as I rolled into the church that my grandfather built, and my mom's advice didn't help. She said, "Don't be telling our business, talking bad about your daddy." As I stepped onto the pulpit, I prayed for God to speak through me, and He did. The words flowed as a voice that I had never heard before emerged from my belly. I spoke of serving in the Navy and transitioning to a drug dealer. Some members became overcome with the Spirit and jumped up and down. My words emitted power. At the close of the service, people said they felt changed and that my words moved them.

I embraced my calling and sought out more engagements. Whenever possible, I spoke at schools and detention centers, hoping to spread my message. All the while, though, God was still working on me. I believe he tested my will so that my current life and not just my past could motivate others. One of those tests came in the form of a man named Ray. I met him while interviewing for nurses. Ray walked into my apartment and gawked as if it were the Taj Mahal. "I live in a trailer in Alabama and can fit it in here," Ray said. I inquired about his experience, and Ray prefaced each response with "boss." Either he's sincere or he's a smooth talker, I thought. Either way, I liked Ray and hired him. Ray performed his job well, but he had a vice I knew too well. Ray was a sex addict. Not a day went by without him discussing sex. Ray spoke of what he had done, what he wanted to do, and how he'd do it. Ray, who was in his 20s, had a propensity for teenage girls. "I don't know how ya'll do it in Alabama," I told him, "but in Georgia, you can get arrested for that." Rather than heeding my warnings, Ray chose to sneak his young conquests in through a back window. It was as if God sent a reflection of my former self and forced me to look in the mirror each day. I loathed what I saw. Ray's actions displayed how I must've appeared during my promiscuous phase. When Ray went on vacation, I called the agency and requested a replacement. Allowing Ray's behavior to continue in my household would've been tantamount to condoning it.

God sent me a vision that I could reach more young people through a non-profit organization. At His prompting, I established the James Brown Youth Empowerment Organization, JBYEO. The nonprofit's purpose is to facilitate an after-school program and provide counseling, peer workshops, and entrepreneurial training. These combined efforts will aid in steering children away from using or selling drugs. I also established James Brown Unlimited, my for-profit speaking business. Eventually, I ceased booking travel reservations to focus all my efforts on my non-profit organization and motivational speaking. I faced financial uncertainty without my travel agency income. Nevertheless, I had learned to trust God's Word. On the day I signed paperwork to register JBYEO, a friend called and told me a fantastical story. She said airplanes had crashed into the Twin Towers. I turned on my television, and in disbelief, I watched the images. Immediately after that tragic event, domestic travel slowed to a grinding halt. I had left the industry just in time.

I continued my quest to motivate young people and made a reenactment video showing my entry into the drug game and the resulting consequences. In order to reach the masses, I needed help, though. I sought out experts who excelled in public speaking and knew that God changed lives. Preachers, I believed, would support my efforts. I then started visiting some of the largest churches in metro-Atlanta. Service after service, I sat in the pews listening to powerful words of inspiration and praise.

Everywhere I went, however, esteemed men of the cloth laughed at my efforts. On one occasion, I handed my reenactment tape to a youth minister. I told him I'd like an opportunity to speak to the congregation's younger members. In God's house, he looked into my eyes and promised to contact me. He never called. On another Sunday at the close of service, I attempted to approach a preacher near the entrance of his office. As I wheeled toward him, his bodyguards abruptly stopped me and closed the door in my face. This wouldn't be the last instance when bodyguards blocked my attempts to speak to a preacher. Jesus walked among his followers and allowed them touch the hem of his garment. These earthly men, nonetheless, felt the need to separate themselves from the masses.

A chance meeting in the fall of 2002 led me to a preacher who cared enough to help. I met an old lady in a grocery store and handed her a business card. I explained the purpose of JBYEO. She suggested I attend a Baptist church in Decatur where the preacher was known for assisting people. Disillusioned by my previous experiences with clergy, I hesitated to follow the lead. The tenth anniversary of my shooting came. For the first time, I returned to the site where Lionel shot me, and ironically, it was now a handicapped parking space. I replayed the night repeatedly and felt a strong urge to attend the reverend's church.

Three days later, I sat amongst his 350-member congregation. When the reverend saw me, he said, "Let me go talk to a friend of mine" and descended the pulpit. He descended from the pulpit and continued, saying, "Glad to see you. How are you doing? A lot of people in your situation stay home and don't get out." We had never met, but the reverend greeted me as a friend. I asked to share my testimony, and he said go right ahead. He snatched my business cards from my splint, looked at one, and said he was going to help me. After I gave my testimony, the reverend said, "We're going to have him speaking in coliseums." With his help, I appeared on a religious television broadcast called the Bobby Hurd Show. Months later, Trinity Broadcasting Network got a copy of my reenactment video and asked me to come on TBN to give my testimony. After the show aired, I received emails from people around the world. They all commented on how my story had moved them. On the Sundays that followed, the reverend would often say to the congregation, "We're going to help James Brown Youth Empowerment Organization."

Over time, things changed. One week when the reverend got sick and couldn't preach, I asked if he'd like me to speak in his place. His response astonished me. "They don't want to hear that," he said. Eight months later, my van broke down. I asked the reverend if he could help me get it repaired. After all, I tithed faithfully. "We don't help people with that," he advised. Although the reverend's demeanor had changed, I appreciated the encouragement he initially provided. Due to my transportation issues, I stopped going to church. Two months later, I ran into a member of the reverend's congregation. She asked how I was feeling and said she had heard I was ill. I told her she was mistaken and that, fortunately, I had been and was quite healthy. She informed me that reverend took up a collection on my behalf. Needless to say, I never received a penny of that money.

The experiences I had at reverend's church and others taught me to be weary of whom I trust with my future. Perhaps my disappointment would've been lessened if I had remembered that those preachers, despite their statures, were simply humans.

Later, I'd met Bennie, a man who preached from the street instead of a pulpit. Everyone called him "Preacha." Bennie stood on street corners with his sound system, spreading the gospel. People stood listening and shouting, "Preach, Preacha." I told Bennie my goals, and he began visiting the prisons and other institutions with me. Together, we rode up and down Interstate 20 in his old clucker. He had humility and sincerity, something that the other preachers lacked. We became friends and partners.

Bennie renewed my faith in mankind. He may not have preached in a well-known church filled with thousands of members, but he worked for God just the same. After connecting with him, I wondered how many people I had passed by – the homeless man on the street, the teenager who bagged my groceries – without giving them a second thought or even acknowledging their presence. Everyone has value and a destiny to fulfill, whether they or others around them realize it.

In 2003, I heard that Les Brown would be in town at a conference. I had to meet the man whose voice beckoned me during my hospital stay. Maybe, I hoped, that at least he'd give me some words of wisdom. I connected with Les and gave him a copy of my promotional package. Les said, "James Brown, you inspire me. You could've given up, but you didn't. I'm going to help you, son." I had learned to skeptically approach offers of assistance, but Les carried out his promise. I started attending his seminars and training classes in order to polish my speaking skills. He's since become a spiritual father of sorts, offering encouragement and advice. There have been times when I wanted to quit, but Les' support and positivity have helped sustain me.

In March of the next year, I reunited with an old girlfriend, Teresa. She was having a difficult time. Teresa had two sons and two daughters. They all lived in one bedroom of her parents' home. Teresa separated from her husband, and he neglected to pay child support. Teresa said that the man she had left me for was physically and verbally abusive. God, I felt, sent me to her. I offered to help in any way possible. Teresa's circumstances were so dire that she couldn't afford lunch. She worked in a daycare and ate off the children's plates. I made sure that Teresa had lunch each day. I tried to show her another side of life. I took her out to dinner, plays, and sporting events. Teresa told me she was celibate and, like me, living for God. Old feelings resurfaced, and I found myself falling for her again. A month later she confessed to having sex with her husband's cousin. The reason she gave was because he offered to buy her some tires.

I wanted to uplift Teresa and show her how real men treat their women. As she shared details of her childhood that were strikingly similar to mine, I felt she needed my emotional support too. Teresa's cousin molested her, and her father abused her mother. Resuming our former relationship, we had sporadic sexual interludes. I wanted to love her pain and low self-esteem away. Sometimes she asked to borrow money. Usually, though, I volunteered to give her money so she could go to the hairdresser or have pocket change. I opened my apartment as a refuge for Teresa and her children, but she hesitated to let me meet the children. In October, Teresa finally introduced us. Her oldest son asked to call me daddy. That tore me up inside because he had a real father who discarded him, and I knew what that felt like. I talked to Teresa's children, read to them and, in general, spent time with them. For Christmas, I bought them bicycles. They wanted to be with me every moment.

In February I returned to Shepherd to have another surgery on my bed sores. This stay lasted 30 days this time. During that period, I let Teresa and her children use my apartment, and she visited the hospital a few times. When I returned home, Teresa seemed guarded and stopped coming by my apartment. "This is déjàvu," I thought, so I stopped taking her calls. I fasted and prayed for three days that God would rid me of the hold Teresa held over me. Two weeks passed before we spoke. After prodding Teresa, she admitted that she was dating someone. Teresa also got a tax refund and money from selling the house she had shared with her husband. She rented an apartment but never invited me to visit. In other words, Teresa didn't need me anymore.

I tried to rekindle an old flame and help Teresa with her issues. In the process, I learned one of the most important lessons of my life, one that took me years to master. The past is for reflection, not reliving. Those who hold on to the past delay their futures. With a clear mind, I focused on my organization and my business. I attended Beulah Heights Bible College and took a thought-provoking class that helped me take my speaking to another level. I learned about introverts, extroverts, and how people think. In the process, I learned a lot about my personality. I've continued seeking out ways to improve myself as a speaker and as a person.

In 2005, I felt as if God dropped a trillion dollars in my lap by prompting me to tell my story through this book and a play titled "What Goes on in Your House, Stays in Your House," which is based on my life. I'm excited when I wake up each day. Due to my paralysis, my morning routine takes an hour and a half to complete. Even so, I don't let my paralysis hold me down. In fact, I've become "handiquipped." Aunt Lillian and the old lady I met in that Atlanta apartment long ago were both right. I've learned to walk again, metaphorically speaking. I lead a more productive and purpose-driven life now than I did before the shooting.

Before I decided to go into business with my dad, I reached a point of hopelessness and despair. As I reflect, my life could've taken many other wrong turns. Thankfully, I didn't become a molester, kill anyone while driving drunk, or end up in prison for selling drugs. My paralysis demonstrated God's mercy because I actually deserved death. The police figured my injury was punishment enough and chose not to prosecute me. There's a reason God stopped that bullet from killing me and stopped Lionel from firing another shot. Through His forgiveness, God wiped my slate clean and allowed me another opportunity to do His will.

Before my uncle M.C. died on January 23, 2004, I shared my dream with him to become a motivational speaker. "Do it and God's gonna bless you," he said. "Stay humble. You've got the voice to touch lives. I don't see how you do it in that wheelchair because I couldn't do it." He was subsequently diagnosed with diabetes-induced gangrene. One of his legs was amputated, forcing him to become wheelchair-bound. M.C. was the umbilical cord to my future, providing the first dose of love that kept me alive. Within a month after the amputation, M.C. died. The man who stopped me from committing suicide without even realizing it, lost his own will to live. M.C. called me his hero because I had the courage to speak out against drugs and use my past as an example. Telling my full life story is something I had to work toward, however, because I had been trained to remain silent about my family life. Now, I know the humility and freedom that rests in disclosing past failures and victories. Not only does one free oneself, but one is also able to free others.

All young people have talents. What many lack, however, is guidance and motivation. I once spoke at Preacha's church in front of a crowd of teenagers. When I finished, a young man who reminded me of my former self approached me. "Thank you," he said. "I needed to hear that. I have an ounce of cocaine in my pocket, and I'm gonna throw it away."

That moment and others like it are what keep me pursuing my vision and what has given me courage in my life's crises.

Five Steps to Reinventing Yourself

Complete the exercises on the following pages. Work the steps in order from 1 to 5. Complete one step at a time. Move on to the next step only after you have resolved the one before it. Find an encouraging friend to help you through each step.

Principle	Proverb	Plan
1. Forgiving	*There is no revenge so complete as forgiveness.* -Josh Billings	1. Forgive yourself 2. Forgive violator(s)
2. Faith	*Trust in the Lord with all your heart and lean not on your own understanding.* -Proverbs 3:5	1. Faith in God 2. Faith in your abilities
3. Finding Purpose	*Do not call to mind former things, or ponder things of the past. Behold, I do something new. Now it will spring forth; will you not be aware of it? I will even make a roadway in the wilderness and rivers in the desert.* -Isaiah 43:18-19	1. Forget your past 2. Forge new goals 3. Forever pray
4. Forward Thinking	*Do all you can with what you have in the time you have in the place you are.* - Nkosi Johnson	1. Fixate on changing only you, no one else 2. Fixate on your goal(s) and using what you have, without becoming blinded by needs.
5. Fighting a Good Fight	*I think a hero is an ordinary individual who finds strength to persevere and endure in spite of overwhelming obstacles.* -Christopher Reeve	1. Find positive allies 2. Find endurance
Goal: **Freedom**	*The last of the human freedoms is to choose one's attitude in any given set of circumstances.* -Victor Frankl	**1. From the past** **2. To try new things** **3. To allow others to be themselves while you be you !**

FORGIVING

There is no revenge so complete as forgiveness.
-Josh Billings

As I searched for a cure for my external condition, God showed me where I most needed healing: my heart. On page 113, you can read where I began my most important life transition: forgiving. Likewise, you should begin your reinvention with this crucial step.

Slaves must serve their masters, and if you are ensnared in hatred, guilt, blame or other negative feelings toward another person or yourself, then it's time to regain your freedom. Take these steps:

Forgive Yourself

List the things you have done to someone else, including God, that causes you negative memories, reactions or emotions:

1. _____

2. _____

3. _____

4. _____

5. _____

6. _____

7. _____

8. _____

9. _____

10. _____

Forgive Violators

List the things others have done to you or someone you love that causes you negative memories, reactions or emotions:

1. _____

2. _____

3. _____

4. _____

5. _____

6. _____

7. _____

8. _____

9. _____

10. _____

After you have completed your list, ask God for forgiveness. If possible, ask the person whom you hurt for forgiveness. Next, forgive yourself. Show yourself the same unconditional love that God shows you and all humanity. Take these same steps for those who have hurt you, excusing them for their wrong. Finally, go about your life as if these situations never occurred.

FAITH

Trust in the Lord with all your heart and
lean not on your own understanding.

-Proverbs 3:5

I didn't know where I was going, but, through faith, I found the courage to move forward. On page 119, you can read where I ventured out into the city with limited physical abilities but great expectations. I found faith in God and the abilities he had given me.

Having faith is more important than having talent, for it opens up possibilities that you have never imagined or dared to try. Finding faith means releasing your fears, doubts and inhibitions to God. You'll need this to gain your new freedom.

Faith in God

List the areas in your life in which courage to act have consistently been a problem:

1. _____

2. _____

3. _____

4. _____

5. _____

What must you remind yourself about what God has promised or done concerning your challenges? In order for you to overcome a challenge, repeat this to yourself every time the situation presents itself.

Faith in Your Abilities

List the things that you are good at doing:

1. _____

2. _____

3. _____

4. _____

5. _____

6. _____

7. _____

8. _____

9. _____

10. _____

God could have given your gifts to anyone else, but He chose you. Ask yourself if you have used any of these abilities to better your life. If not, what can you do to begin using them to better your life or someone else's?

FINDING PURPOSE

Do not call to mind former things, or ponder things of the past. Behold, I do something new. Now it will spring forth; will you not be aware of it? I will even make a roadway in the wilderness and rivers in the desert.
-Isaiah 43:18-19

When the "not guilty" verdict came in for the man who shot me, I had several choices. Among them, I could have become resentful and stagnant. On page 121, you can read where I made the decision to find my purpose despite all else.

Finding purpose is when your life begins. This can occur at any point, stage or age, but it must occur in order to become fulfilled. The first step toward fulfillment is forgetting what has blocked it: your past failures. No one can change your past, not even God. However, God can use our past as a means and a ministry. You can too, so use your past as a springboard or a guide.

Forget Your Past

Determine what you have learned from your most memorable mistakes:

1. _____

2. _____

3. _____

4. _____

5. _____

6. _____

7. _____

Forge New Goals

What are your short-term life goals?

1. _____

2. _____

3. _____

4. _____

5. _____

What are your long-term life goals?

6. _____

7. _____

8. _____

9. _____

10. _____

FORWARD THINKING

Do all you can with what you have
in the time you have in the place you are.

-Nkosi Johnson

As I lay in my hospital bed, I heard Les Brown say something that changed my outlook on life. I couldn't change my state or the people around me, but I could change the only thing I eternally control: my attitude. On page 135, you can read where I decided to use my voice to inspire positive change in others who suffered the same fate as me: a poor attitude.

Forward thinking begins as soon as you stop looking or thinking backward. The last exercise involved looking back. This one involves curing backward thinking. The first step in gaining forward thinking is realizing that you can only change you, no one else. You can, however, speak and act in ways to inspire change in others, but the decision to change is ultimately theirs. Therefore, stop focusing on everything that you can't change: other people and the past. The only thing left is you and your future.

Change Only You

What changes must you make to step out of another person's life and regain yours?

1. _____

2. _____

3. _____

4. _____

5. _____

Change Your Outlook

List the excuses you have used to sidetrack your determination from reaching your destiny:

_____

_____

_____

_____

How can you achieve your short-term goals using the resources that you have or can get?

1. _____

2. _____

3. _____

4. _____

5. _____

How can you achieve your long-term goals using the resources that you have or can get?

6. _____

7. _____

8. _____

9. _____

10. _____

FIGHTING A GOOD FIGHT

I think a hero is an ordinary individual who finds strength to persevere and endure in spite of overwhelming obstacles.

-Christopher Reeve

After a preacher in a pulpit failed me, God sent me a preacher without pride or a pulpit. On page 138, you can read when I met a man who renewed my faith in friends. I needed him at the time to help me move forward. Similarly, we all need other people, but we must be selective. To find supportive friends, we must allow God to put people in and out of our lives. Some friendships are only for a season while others are for a lifetime.

Fighting a good fight involves both "support and endurance." When we get tired or discouraged, we will need both factors in order to continue. Endurance or perseverance comes naturally for some but must be summoned in others. Nevertheless, we can fight and win with the right tools. The first step is surrounding yourself with winners. These allies can provide support and inspiration for the endurance you'll need to win.

Find Positive Allies

Who are the most positive, supportive people in your life?

1. _____

2. _____

3. _____

4. _____

5. _____

6. _____

7. _____

Once you've identified these people, spend more time talking with them about your goals. If you have no one or very few people, ask God to add real friends and supporters to your life. Remember, friends aren't people who only tell you what you want to hear. They are people who tell you what you need to hear.

Find Endurance

What causes you discouragement and fear?

1. _____

2. _____

3. _____

4. _____

5. _____

What *must* you do to rid yourself of discouragement and fear?

1. _____

2. _____

3. _____

4. _____

5. _____

You'll need encouragement and determination to reach your goals. Prayer is an essential tool for this. God provides recovery, revelation and resolve. Ask Him.

GOAL: FREEDOM

The last of the human freedoms is to choose one's attitude
in any given set of circumstances.

-Victor Frankl

As you go through the steps on the previous pages, pray each day and fill in the *questions*:

Lord, give me the courage to fail (*at what?*), forgive (*who?*), find (*why?*), fight (*when?*), and forge ahead (*where?*). In Jesus' name, Amen.

Printed in the United States
108316LV00004B/175-222/A